# Head in Heaven

by Barbro Curman

www.lightspira.com

Published by LightSpira, Sweden
www.lightspira.com

ISBN 978-91-86613-07-5
First issue, 2011

Author: Barbro Curman
www.neweranet.org

Cocreators:
Åsa Rosén, art design
Fabian Björnstjerna, photographs
Jenny Widingsjö, photo postproduction
Marie Örnesved, LightSpira, editing
Kim Farnell, proof reading
Recito Förlag/Förlagsservice.se, book design

# Head in Heaven
# Feet on the Ground
# Hands in Society

*To my husband Mikael*
*with love*

# Prologue

This book reflects one woman´s spiritual journey. It is a way for me to forward the flaming torch that was given to me further to you and to others who may recognise themselves in my story. It is a story meant to encourage all of you who are longing to intensify your own inner journeying.

Some people might find the whole idea of experiencing an inner guide as strange. They might even claim that I have invented the whole thing, based on my need to heal myself. Today this does not matter to me. I know the truth deep inside, and I have had the privilege to also share with a few people, who from their own experiences understand my knowing. What matters, and is of importance, is what came out of it. "You know him by his fruit" is an old truth.

From a scientific point of view, what do we know? My inner knowing tells me that we are all co-creators with life. We are just conscious of it to different levels.

Last summer I read a fabulous book by Lynne McTaggart. She has been patiently gathering high quality research over a period of thirty years concerning how our thoughts influence other people and how they also seemingly influence the material world. She points to a concept that the researchers call the "Zero Point Field". This is a field of potential from which human thoughts co-create on a quantum level.

This is to me, a Gestalt Therapist since the 1970s, very confirming. Already in around 1920-30 Kurt Lewin had created what he called the "Field Theory", an early variation of system theory.

This theory concerns how a pattern takes form within a field (system) and the process of change that follows. This theory is widely used as a basis in organisational and personal development within the Gestalt theory and methodology.

What if great spirits like Mother Mary, Jesus Christ, Buddha, Mohammed and many, many others influenced the zero point field so that there is a *potential* for us human beings to attract universal love, wisdom etc.?

What if our commitment as human beings is about *true intention* beyond our fears, doubts and other covers-ups? The old habit of *praying* seems to me to be neglected in today's society. Maybe we do not pray in a compassionate and true way until we are in despair for some reason? Maybe we forget to pray just to thank God and life for all our gifts?

To pray in thankfulness is to open our hearts. Then, and only then, do we attract the potential from the zero point field, although the possibilities were there all the time.

Every spiritual journey is unique, as is every human soul. There are however milestones along the path that are similar between us, but they are just like stones of inspiration. No one can know for another human being. Wisdom is within each one of us, hidden in our body-mind-soul-spirit and the connecting wholeness.

Today we face a time in our history when we as human beings are on the way to destroying our beautiful home, our planet. It is urgent that as many as possible of us focus in our hearts and passion taking us beyond our survival strategies based on fear. The time has gone for solving our huge problems through fighting each other physically or psychologically, as it will only turn into a terrifying boomerang.

"It is of great value when one person is focusing her intent from a pure heart and when 4-5 people or more are doing it together then great changes are happening in the world." Those words come from the famous anthropologist Margaret Mead.

We are many today realising that if there are enough gatherings with the intention of open and loving hearts, then the critical mass is enough to save the world. This is holistic thinking and how change actually occurs. Just look at the systems of mobiles and the world wide web! Who would have foreseen this rapid change thirty or forty years ago?

I have *hope!* And I have *faith!* And certainly - what opened me up was *love,* a love beyond desires. My first lesson was to dare *receive* that kind of love, later to let it pour within in me and further out into the world.

Already Jesus said: *"Faith, hope and love - these three, but greatest of them all is love."*

Love is what keeps our universe together.

Mallorca, October 6, 2009.
Barbro Curman

# Completion and a new beginning

*Stockholm June 13, 2009.*

"Yesterday, my heart was burning. Today my whole body is burning," I said, totally overwhelmed. In that state of mind I could not move. This was like nothing I had experienced before.

"She is being over-shadowed," I heard my friend Doris say. Doris is one of those special people, who has the gift to see beyond this physical world. I thought I did not have that gift as I do not see auras. What had happened to me during the last five years had however opened my mind to totally new dimensions.

"The heat is coming out to all in the group," I said and felt that it was meant to be. What I experienced was a completion of five years of intense inner personal guidance and by that a manifestation of what this group of people was committed to.

From that day on both my guide and I were free to continue on different paths within our respective dimensions. It meant to me to apply my inner covenant in the everyday, physical life.

What had been an extremely personal inner guidance, now shifted into energies of another kind.

You might think that I would consider "losing" my guide a loss and that I would mourn. Instead I felt lighter and happier than ever, like a bird given leave to fly further. It was like completing a task that had to be completed. The journey is powerful and this was a point of no return.

To complete something is the start of something new. My guidance is now coming from other sources, for example teachings from some great ancient female teachers. I consider those to be of extreme value. The school within another dimension, which my guide brought me to, has become my spiritual home.

A wonderful summer by the sea became like a long breathing out after this event and from the intense work as an organisational consultant which I did parallel to my inner journeying. However, to rest was not enough. I realised that I had to trace the learning patterns of this wisdom treasure given to me. I have actually been on a five year long training camp involving all of my body-mind-soul-spirit and I have received deep wisdom.

When you receive a gift like this, you get it for a reason. There is responsibility along with the gift. The whole idea is to integrate what you have got with the skills and possibilities you have in your physical life, so that you can bring the wisdom further in a practical way. The other dimensions need your hands and feet, your senses, your intellect and mind. I have always been a kind of bridge-builder between worlds, so here I am!

While writing this I recall a session with Doris already in April 2004 when she said to me: "He is putting a leather briefcase next to you. He says that you completed step one when working together in your physical lives and now it is time for steps two and three."

At that time I was exhausted after what you might call "the dark night of the soul". My life was in a great shift. I had left everything I had built in my working life over thirty years and there was illness in my family. The last thing I wanted was more responsibility. What I did not know then was how much support, love and nourishment that I would be given when taking on this inner task. Actually it was not a duty, it was the true meaning of my life and a great treasure. Thank God that my guide was so persistent and kept on knocking at my door until I got the message.

*"You need to understand yourself first and you need to take time to do this"*, a voice said inside me. True! New learning is about getting new perspectives.

So it happened that I decided to go to Mallorca for two weeks in the autumn of 2009, prolonging the summer, to be on my own and above all study my almost daily notes from the five years' intense inner journeying.

I invite you to join me in my tracing for wisdom patterns in what I have been taught. I know that we all need these tools today in different parts of the society. We face a whole new world with totally new challenges. It will no longer work to keep on doing what we have always done. We need to learn how to be our own creators *together* with life itself instead of working against life.

It takes practice to learn and I have been on a five year long training camp learning new skills involving body-mind-soul-spirit. All of it! There are similar learning possibilities for everyone.

# Twelve days in Mallorca

## - Worlds within Worlds -

# 1.

# The calling

I am finally on my way and am at Madrid airport waiting at the gate to board the plane to Palma, Mallorca. The pattern of going away now and then to spend some time alone has begun again. Everyday life is often so intense that I can't hear the little voice from inside; there is too much disturbance. That does not mean that there is anything wrong with everyday life, quite the contrary, but I think most people need a break every now and then to be in silence.

The vague feeling of longing has been my inner lighthouse. It has been stronger during those times when I have gone off track, and also during times when I have been at the gate to a new stage in my life journey. My inner longing has intensified on those occasions and I have had to take action of some kind, or I would have been untrue to myself. The process was tougher when I was younger. Now I know more and I respond without waiting too long.

The very special inner journey that I am now about to tell you about began five years ago. I had started to make daily notes of what was happening in my life. I remember taking my first stumbling steps towards listening to my inner voice and when I now read my notes I recall the whole situation. I woke up hearing a clear and urgent voice saying, ***"TELL THY TRUTH!"***

It was very early in the morning and I was in our lovely summer cottage by the shore of the Swedish west coast. My husband was sleeping beside me. The call was persistent and I took my brand new notebook and went to another room to be by myself. I remember asking myself: "What is this?"

Then I remembered the dream from which I had woken that morning. I was one of many prisoners walking in a very hot desert. We were chained together and had chains around our necks. I could clearly see the iron rings. Every one of us had our hands and feet tightly bound. My surroundings that morning were beautiful and in sharp contrast to my dream and inner state of mind. I was full of despair as I did not want to face the truth of what people did to each other. I was crying but without tears. What could I do? What can a single woman do about the cruelty and ignorance that has always been an integral part of us human beings? The voice returned. ***"TELL THY TRUTH!"***

I realised that there has always been part of my life that I have hesitated to share with others. Why? I guess I was afraid of being ridiculed, afraid of being looked at in a critical and scornful way. I was afraid that my inner treasures would be destroyed. That was, of course, due to the doubtful and critical part of me. I was a capable, organised woman, soon to be sixty years old, and used to keeping things together, both in my family and my working life. Like many people, I was afraid of losing control, despite all the years I'd spent in the therapy and organisational development businesses.

That morning I cried out in despair and was heard. Along with the words: *"Tell thy truth!!!"* came a wave of heat into my solar plexus. That heat gave me strength and hope. It was time to make crucial life decisions!

*"Sing your song – your own,"* the voice reminded me during the next two nights. And I received instructions as to how I could start organising a new professional life now I had left everything that I had been part of building and leading for thirty years.

Here I am now at Madrid airport several years later. In my heavy suitcase, besides some books that are dear to me, are all my handwritten notebooks dating back to that first night in July 2004. I had to pay for excess baggage but I knew it was worth every Swedish krona.

Sitting here by the gate I again hear an inner voice: *"Maybe your fear is heavier than your books?"* Sometimes this voice is just too much to the point. Quite correct! How come that I still fear sharing my spiritual life with others?

I bring to mind one of my earliest childhood memories. I was sitting in my room with the huge family Bible in front of me. Although I was only four or five years old I was fascinated by the book, its size, the special drawings in it and mystical air around it. This was the first time I'd heard an unexpected inner voice. It came clearly from my left side, like it was coming out of the wall. There were no real words, just a loving wordless presence. Already, as a little child, I knew that this was the presence of Jesus Christ.

Although I am privileged, coming as I do from a loving and open family, I did not share this experience with anyone, until I met the person I used to call my spiritual brother. I was thirty and he was thirty-five. There was a special connection between us that was the foundation for almost thirty years of creative work together. He died in October, 2003. Five of us were with him at the time. When he took his last breath, there was light in the room. It felt as if a bird had been set free.

My thoughts return to airport practicalities and my need to show a ticket to prove that I had paid for the extra weight at Stockholm airport. I start worrying that my suitcase won't arrive in Palma. It is again this need for control! Suddenly, I see the smiling face of my spiritual brother. "Oh, you brought your camping wagon!" he said as he looked at my big suitcase. He himself was carrying hardly more than a plastic bag.

It is interesting how dealing with small details like a ticket can grow into such an important matter. Being the good girl I am, I showed my ticket as I reached the first place in line. The woman at the desk just looked at it and tore it apart. So much for its importance.

Yesterday had been a strange day. In the morning I finished planning a crisis management seminar for managers. I went to the office to say goodbye to my colleagues and I got warm hugs and good wishes for my trip to Mallorca. On the quiet street outside the office a car zoomed by at extreme speed, driving against the red light and being chased by a police car. I was a couple of metres away from being hit and so was another woman. We looked at each other. There had been a spectacular helicopter robbery in Stockholm the day before where they'd entered a deposit vault from the roof of a building. My guess was that there was a link. I imagined how people could have been killed by this car. What if a child had stepped out? What kind of world is this? Surely enough, just a couple of blocks ahead, they crashed. I was in shock and walked the streets like a zombie.

My mobile rang. "Coming tomorrow? I will pick you up at the airport and drive you to Puerto de Andratx."

"Do you really have time?" I asked my friend Johannes, who was working as a doctor in his private practice in Palma. "Of course."

The contrast was so huge that warm tears came. I was still trembling, when I returned home to my husband Mikael. I was frozen, touched, and eager to tell him what had happened. We shared a nice dinner. Then I disappeared into a state between sleep and meditation. As I had so many other times during the last five years, I woke up filled with a new, fresh energy and ready to pack.

Later that night I couldn't sleep. A new wave of energies came to me and a voice said: *"Don´t forget that you are carried!"* Those words made me totally calm. I slept for two or three hours and was ready to go. Again I learnt that I am taken care of. My task is to make myself available and inspire others to do the same. The rest is cared for by life itself.

I am finally in Puerto de Andratx, Mallorca! What a gift to be here. I am on what for a couple of weeks I can consider to be, "my" terrace. There is a big flower growing there (called a bougainvillea) with magenta coloured flowers that are like honey to your eyes. When I sent a text message to the woman from whom I was renting the apartment, and thanked her for her welcome, I also asked if there was anything I should take special care of. "Nothing right now, except please, just water the flower!" was her answer. I am myself like a flower needing water. Two months of hard work. Now it is time to be still, enjoy, listen to the silence and open myself for what life wishes to tell me. And to day by day to read all my notebooks and trace the wisdom I have been taught.

Today I found a little beach just five minute's walk away, and enjoyed the sunset close to the special lighthouse at the harbour. I have also been walking to the village at the other end of the harbour to buy fresh fruits and vegetables grown on the island.

While sitting on my terrace in the evening I can see the water, the lights from the other side and all the boats going in and out. I hear the beautiful sound of a flute far away. I feel safe and at home already. I have the time I need to be alone and I don´t feel lonely as I often used to earlier in my life. *"Don´t forget that you are carried!"* the voice repeats to me again. And that is true. The words vibrate within me and I feel like I am surrounded by soft hands. Gratefully, I receive.

I reflect on this beautiful flower on my terrace and how we human beings receive our water of life. Today I have been watered from my inner source several times; it's like bathing in mild, but strong energies. I became electrified throughout my whole body - or rather bodies. These energies act on me like photosynthesis does to flowers. They create a force field between heaven and earth keeping us alive.

My physical body has changed immensely through my last years receiving of high frequencies energies by allowing them into all the energy centres (chakras), and also into the parts of me holding resistance and blockages from old patterns. I am lighter, happier and more creative and I feel like I am walking around in my daily life from a place of light and joy. Maybe this sounds like a fairy tale; still, it is true. Other people notice as well from the outside.

Of course, it has not always happened in such a natural way. This is what my "training camp" was about. To develop skills you need to practice. If you want to be a good flute player and create the nice music that I heard from the terrace, it takes training. Many people practise hearing their inner guidance, but in different ways. This is the profound meaning behind yoga and many spiritual paths in different cultures. People in the old days went to mystery schools in order to practice and learn.

In my case it happened right in the middle of a busy working life. I'd been a mother and a grandmother in a big family and a wife for twenty-five years. I am so thankful for this gift! To be in your daily life and learn how to be true to that inner seed within you, your blueprint, I believe is a challenge and at the same time a beautiful gift to all of us.

When a few friends and I founded what is now The Gestalt Academy of Scandinavia in 1976, we made "Head in Heaven, Feet on the Ground, Hands in Society" our slogan. The divine energies are not only for you or me to dwell in. They are meant to inspire concrete work in the physical world to help us to heal and develop our society, our planet and ourselves as human beings.

Again I recall the summer of 2004. That was when I felt my first impulses towards taking the journey that I am now on. I have already mentioned the first words that came to me: *"Tell thy truth!"* Along with these inner experiences books "happened" to come in my hands, becoming like teachers. That summer the book "Secret of Shambhala" by James Redfield was in the bookshop in the little town close to our summer cottage. And a box of pencils in different colours was waving to me. So I bought both. My legs almost walked themselves from the food shop to the bookshop, as if they were saying to me: *"There is more to life than having a good meal."* This was the day before I woke up from that dream in the desert. What stood out to me was what they called "The Field of Prayer". My inner longing was to discover how I could be a constructive tool in today's world. This had been my heartfelt intention long before I read this book.

The book said:

- First extension: When you are clear about your intention, you build energy by connecting to your Higher Self.
- Second extension: Conscious awareness, being alert of synchronicity.
- Third extension: The contagious consciousness of influencing the Higher Self of others.
- Fourth extension: Daring to have faith that the human world is able to get closer to Shambhala. Keep our high vibrations/frequencies also when facing fear and hostility. The wish and ability to surrender to and recognise the dekinas/angels is necessary.

Why is that necessary, you may ask? When you believe that a loving force exists then you are able to ask for help, to surrender. You need to *ask* for help to be able to *get* help. As human beings, we are not allowed to intervene in each other's lives unless we are invited to. Angels and other divine beings are invited by our longing.

I start reading from my notebook. Again I see the link between what is said there and what is needed for organisations at this time on earth. The words coming to me were: *Leadership in the New Era - the power of trust.* Little did I know then that I had received the title of my business book that would be published in 2008.

My inner guidance provides further important details of directions: *"Dare to have faith even against and beyond your own personal experience. Dare to address the higher self within my enemies or within those whom I worry about. Make decisions in a state of trust, confirming the living as opposed to decisions based on survival coming from fear. Teach this to managers and other leaders because they influence so many people."*

This is a day for me and my husband Mikael to be quietly together. It is our last summer weekend in our cottage. I am again reading the book, "Anna, Grandmother of Jesus" – a wonderful inspiration of many dimensions, containing spiritual, historical and esoteric wisdom. This book awakens my longing for deepening and continuing my inner path. Thank you Aniesa for giving it to me at the right time!

I experience a strong meditation later that same afternoon, the sea, the light over the sea. A soft and still strong energy is coming to me – as an opening towards light in my forehead and my head.

Looking in my notes I see a drawing of a tall light figure approaching my head and forehead with a kind of light beam. The sea makes a border to the picture.

I remember being awake almost all night. There was so much energy within me. It was time to express it in some way. What form? How should I communicate? Through different situations illustrating the power of trust? How personal should I dare to be? What am I afraid of? What about my faith? Thinking about how many books already exist, I wonder, why me? Am I able to? And *yes,* I have things to tell! – I have pricking sensations all over my hand. I have to drop the pen. I get the picture that my hands are supposed to be used for healing. Instead of writing? I don´t know…

What I did not understand until years later was that I had been given light energy directly into my two hands, so that they would be able to guide me beyond my intellect. My notes say that I was receiving answers to all my questions that night by taking notes from the book I was reading. But what is actually meant by strange words like "initiation"? In the old days, mystery school tales say that disciples went through scary things, like tests. This is not how we do things today. Life itself has enough challenges if we are open to receive and learn from them. So when I read this definition I felt fine with it. "Initiation is an experience from inside that takes us over a threshold of a change that is not possible to return from."

Another important statement: "It is simply a matter of choosing to be more aware of where you are placing your attention! The threshold is about trusting that we all have a spark of God within ourselves. From that part of us we are able to love all that lives, also our own shadow parts."

Five years later I read this in my notebook and notice how today my whole body is electric like a transformation system, where the different pieces are linked to one another. My arms and legs, throat and cheeks loosen up step by step, and it happens in connection with the energies from the other chakras. I have asked for release of tension, so that I can be the vessel for creation I am meant to be.

How far this first action of trust in the summer of 2004 has brought me! And it is true that there is no way back, only forward, and I am very happy about that fact.

# 2.

# The knocking

I slept many hours that night, like a long breathing out. Now I am settled and ready for whatever might happen. This time in Mallorca I have decided not to rent a car as I need to be in a situation where I do not have to worry about anything practical, like finding my way or driving where there are heights. I am terrified of heights.

Yesterday when I booked a session with the osteopath Juan Carlos in Palma I recalled a session I'd had with him six years earlier. While his sensitive hands mildly released tensions in my body, I visualised with deep fear some of these needle curves of the mountains of Mallorca. Now we have three sessions planned during my stay. Perfect! I will need them.

Today is a warm and slightly foggy morning. When I woke up around ten, I meditated in my terrace chair overlooking the beautiful flower and the harbour. After giving thanks for the guidance and my surrender to the divine plan, I received energies coming from both "heaven and earth" as I call them. It is not as mystical as it may sound. We human beings are kept on this earth through gravity (earth) and another source of energy comes from our sun or beyond (heaven). We are like human flowers or trees integrating these forces as best we can.

We have, unlike animals, our free will. This means that we are able to reflect and make choices. So we as human beings are partly like animals with survival instincts and partly divine beings, linked to the divine spark within. There is nothing wrong per se with survival instincts, for example, the need for physical security, sex and power. They however need guidance from a wiser part of us. This need is often misunderstood and turned into ascetic living, sexual denial or hidden ways to use your power. Surrender and submission are complete opposites.

The key is *love.* "Hug your shadow", is a title of a good book about this. "Peep secretly with tenderness at yourself," I used to say when working with people or myself. Our inner critical self causes the dilemma, not the part of us receiving the accusing finger.

I had a strong impulse to just go inside and receive. Something was moving my hip and I could hardly walk. A voice came: *"This is a preparation. Every attempt you make to run ahead of the now - you are blocking the flow. You are being trained to become a total receiver, like a vessel. Your whole body is changing. Great things are happening."*

My answer came immediately: "Show me the way. My intention is clear and I know I have obstacles."

The voice continued: *"You have been scared of letting other people, especially men, carry you, so you chose men who were themselves afraid of carrying others. You have received a lot as an earthly woman but this is about male and female energies on a universal level. That is why you need to let us carry you. From this union we create what we call the "light body", which is actually your extended aura, your electromagnetic force field."*

A teaching on a bodily level followed. I have long been told to keep my focus in my forehead and crown and not to interfere. To just let what is happening happen with my awareness. My early training of body and sensory awareness has truly been of great help. I was finally able to let go of the striving and excitement and just let myself be carried from within. Soft, warm tears of joy and happiness came with the knowledge that this was new to me at this deep level. When I woke up from receiving, my hip was soft as was my whole body.

I go through my notes and see a big gap. How come? I recall coming home from our summer cottage to start up my own little office after quitting my job. I was preparing a homepage reflecting the new situation. Mikael (who is also a Gestalt therapist) and I kept working together with therapy groups and couple therapy, like we had been doing for over twenty years. There was however a sudden ending to our professional life together. In October 2004, Mikael was diagnosed with lung cancer after being a heavy smoker for fifty years. Death was knocking at our door. His attitude that, "I´m not living to cure cancer, I´m here to *live,*" I believe was healing. He, of course, was helped by skilled doctors and professional treatment too. Today, there are no signs of cancer, although the journey has been tough. We have both learnt to be thankful for the days we have, not knowing about the future. But who knows about the future?

On December 26, 2004, the tsunami in Asia came as a shock to the world. There were a lot of Swedes killed on their holidays in Thailand. Most Swedish people knew someone who had died there or who had lost dear ones. The search for people in Thailand was ongoing while Mikael was in surgery to take out his left lung. I remember that morning clearly. I stayed in bed with my telephone beside me, waiting for the doctors to call. At that moment I was happy to have learnt something about how to link to higher energies. I held a space for Mikael within me. I visualised the operating theatre and the doctors. A voice told me: "*Stay where you are, you are not supposed to be in the same room.*" I stayed and sent my love and prayers, understanding that dealing with life and death is, of course, beyond my abilities. The telephone rang after a couple of hours and at the other end of the line was a proud and happy doctor.

A young couple, friends of our family, were on honeymoon in Thailand with a child growing in her womb. They were all killed. How little we know! To lose a child, a sister, a brother or a mate – is it possible to live with that and still find meaning in life?

At home we learned to cope with our new situation. I enjoyed my new little office and made new business connections. I kept doing my meditation, I gave myself support and further training in meeting the energies, but I did not write anything. The inside knockings became stronger and stronger. Strange things happened, like the electricity went off, a TV went on by itself, my mobile behaved as never before or after. It showed time after time the heartbeat curve and a word kept coming onto the screen: *Outdoors!*

Finally, I understood and made a decision: "I need to be silent for a few days." I phoned a couple who were friends of mine and who I knew would understand. They offered to let me stay in their little guest house in the countryside.

The only thing I took with me was a gift from a friend who might have understood what was going on. It was a kind of map that showed the energy body points that you can unlock if you so wish and if you are ready. So it happened that my kundalini (the channel of energy moving through our spines) was opened. So simple in one way, and yet I was stunned. I had been reading books about this. I had years of body therapy behind me, but this was different. There was humour and joy in it, it's hard to describe. I wrote in my diary, *THANKS!!* I had become mute, maybe that was one of the reasons why this happened? Anyway, it was a great gift! I have learnt that I can trust my inner guidance whatever. It is all there, when I trust my intuition and follow my path.

Today is such a beautiful morning, sun, blue sky.... Maybe time to look out into the world? I remember driving my car the four hundred kilometres back to Stockholm. It took all my awareness to stay in the now and be alert. I heard a voice from my guide: *"Your responsibility is the physical part, using your arms and legs, your senses and your intellect. We take care of the rest."* I arrived safely home and a new chapter in my life began.

I had to get used to these powerful energies flowing within me and being able to live my everyday life at the same time. I performed my work and I functioned better than ever. Still it was like I was living in two worlds. Thank God that I had close friends like Gunilla who knew more about this than me.

In the mornings I meditated and I learned how to stabilise the "light tube" or "light pillar" as it is usually called in esoteric literature. One morning, when the kundalini went through me again, a voice said: "*Cumpleaños!*" (happy birthday in Spanish). I was truly a beginner in the Spanish language, still there it was. I had taken another step on my journey - an initiation into the next level.

My friend Doris, not knowing what had happened to me, said in one of her readings, "It is like you walk around and then you suddenly stand still reflecting on what is actually happening." Very true.

I was travelling one day on the Stockholm underground. On the opposite side of the train I saw an Indian woman. She was beautiful and was wearing a traditional elegant sari. I had never seen anything like this on the Stockholm underground, although we host many people from other countries. The woman looked at me as if she was able to see my aura, and I felt she could. She smiled in a gentle and friendly way. Then, at the next stop, she left the train looking back at me, smiled again and waved to me. And just as Doris had said, I was in wonder. What was happening to me? I still wonder if that woman was of flesh and blood. It was like she had come from another time and space to support me.

I receive another round of energies this afternoon. The morning was about preparation. Now it was time to be on the spot. Gradually, this inner link has turned into a covenant. This is serious business and I have to be clear about what I am willing to say yes and no to. This doesn´t mean to always live up to things, it only means to be true from the bottom of my heart. When I am afraid, I ask for help to continue to be true to my heart.

In the same moment as I confirmed my inner commitment, I heard three sharp bangs of thunder. Of course this thunder, and later the lightning, was there anyway, but to me it was a confirmation.

No wonder I needed to go to Mallorca to face my fears. Along the path I had grown to the point when it was up to me to be able to keep the bridge and stay clear with my yes and no. It was also my responsibility to do my best to clear the way from old blockages.

The energies keep teaching me. The little tea candle in its box, has just burnt out. It is half past three in the morning and it had been alight since I went to bed at midnight. I have been in a state between meditation and sleep. The energies often come to me like this, when I am not fully awake, like before falling asleep or early in the mornings. In fact I have often the feeling that my guides are doing a lot of work with me, while I am asleep. I guess it is easier to reach me then when there is less disturbance and control on my part. It is well known that many people get their most creative ideas at those times, receiving a solution that was impossible to find the day before. The intellect is good for us to have, of course, but it is the same as survival instincts; it makes a good servant but not a good master. Who is the master then? Our master is to me the divine spark within each of us. When we listen to that spark, it becomes like a navigator in all kinds of stormy weathers. I think most people know the difference from inside. It is just an issue of deepening that knowledge if we so desire.

I truly enjoy now having, as it seems, endless time to just be and listen to my navigator second by second. When I woke up from this meditation or half sleep, I realised that I had received a kind of structure for this book and that I also received the message in English, not in Swedish. To me this pointed to another form of publishing. The message I got was that what I am doing now is a kind of fundamental work of structuring the wisdom I have received. And that later this inspiration will flow also to other books more directly linked to leadership and organisational development, as well as to lectures and seminars. Again, I experience how much inspiration I get when I open myself to receive these light energies. It really is like being a co-creator with life itself. I could never sit there thinking this up intellectually. Often,

I get totally new perspectives that turn my conventional thinking upside down. Later these are always shown to be very creative.

Receiving light in this strong way was not on my agenda until I was taught how to. And sometimes the teacher comes from an unexpected source.

One day, for once alone in the cottage, I am slowly dancing to a special song "Anthem" by Leonard Cohen. "There is a crack, a crack in everything, that´s how the light gets in... ...Ring a bell that still can ring - forget your perfect offering..."

It is amazing how this poet had become to me like a spiritual teacher. Those words made me understand how receiving light and love is beyond my control. The "crack", however dark it may seem, becomes the receiver of light. If we were all as polished and perfect (whatever that is?) as gemstones, there would be no receiver. Often we try to be perfect as a cover-up to stop us from getting what we need - love! We need to ask for light and love with an honest pure heart; otherwise we do not get it. We have our free will, we can be shown to the water but no one can drink it for us. That is our own choice.

What I also learnt from this song was how to breathe, while receiving. It was like I was told *"Let it in! Allow it to come in!"* instead of *"Breathe it in!"* The light and love came *between* my breaths. It was like holding the space in the now for it to happen and not interfering with it by acting in any way. My part was to keep my intention and my faith that love and light was there for me.

It came naturally to me as I, as a Gestalt therapist, had been trained to be precisely in the *now* with awareness, and to let the wisdom of life be its master. I recall being interviewed by a Swedish daily newspaper in the late 1980s. "Does Gestalt teach spirituality?" the journalist asked me. I remember answering what also became the finish of the article. "We never tell people what to believe in, that is up to them. However, the intense work with conscious awareness of body-mind-senses often inspires people to go further along their spiritual path. And many do." I used to look upon myself as a kind of "cleaning lady" assisting people while they are cleaning their communication antennas.

When my thoughts go back to the time when I learnt how to breathe and bring in light in my body, I realise that I took some very important decisions to preserve my own life force. My old pattern of easily going into organising and becoming over responsible had shown its face again and again. It was an old habit but I discovered it much sooner than in my younger days. This pattern is also a part of me. Our life patterns are like themes in a symphony with variations. They are just different.

When I stand strong in my own life force, then the outer world is manifested around that. It so happened that I understood that the intention was to create a kind of network organisation based on the vision: *"The aim is to create meeting points for people working in different fields in society. What they share is a longing to be able to work in a way so that the force of life is sustained."* Again, reading my notes, I realise that I, by being true to myself and my own life, received inspiration how to build organisations in the coming new era.

Inside, I was saying goodbye to a time in my life when I had been a mother figure, both at home and as a leader of organisations. Everyone is independent now, and it is time for me to focus on my own spiritual journey. I am enjoying my morning meditation on the other side of the small peninsula. Today, it came strongly to me, how love opens your heart and the greatest gift is to be able to *feel* that love in a pure way when receiving. Then the highest within me is with me, when it flows from my forehead, through my spine, down into earth and up again.

I had a morning swim, fresh and nice, just before the rain came. It feels good to go back to bed, enjoying my breakfast. I am also getting ideas from inside how to write.

I recall a voice saying to me: *"You have got a jewel in your hand – your task is to grind it. You influence other people from that jewel."*

While receiving that, my left hand spontaneously gave support and warmth to my right hand. It was a calm and rainy day. I received a lot of light. Later that day I heard the same voice as the day before: *"Lay your hand in mine, put your elbow in mine."* There was surrender from my right arm into my left.

I showed Mikael the map of how to unlock energy points. I experienced in his body the place where his lung had been. It was deserted, empty and dark. It needed love, warmth and light. As I received love from within, I let it flow further to him!

Back at my terrace in Mallorca, it is cooler than yesterday, but it is still wonderful to be able to sit outside. The rain stopped in the afternoon while I was walking from the village at the other side of the harbour. It has been an intense day in my inner life. Reading my notes from the first year of my journey, I realise that my inner guidance is coming to me in a new way today. I am receiving it just as strong and loving as before, but not in a personal way. It is like I am aware of my own higher self working together with my guide on another level, while I, in my physical body, am here receiving guidance from both. It strikes me that spiritual growth is similar to the growth of a child into adulthood. At that time I needed a hand in mine to keep the connection and help me not to lose track. Today I have been trained, so I recognise what is given to me.

*"This is how you make contact and raise your energies"*, the voice told me today. *"Don´t misuse it! It is now up to you to contact us."*

"So it is time for me to stand on my on two spiritual legs now," I thought. "Am I ready for this?"

3.

# The bridge is being confirmed

I woke up at nine thirty, refreshed after a long night sleep and prepared to meet a new day. Some rain had fallen in the morning, but now the sun was coming out from behind the clouds. The rain and thunder was over for now.

There are many ways to spread a message. Today I have been reading Dan Brown´s latest book, "The Lost Symbol". You could read this as yet another fictional story. However, I was excited about how Washington DC is described as being filled with ancient symbols from the esoteric traditions of Egypt and other old cultures. Somehow I feel connected when I read about these cultures and other lineages that followed. The formal power in society has always been suspicious of philosophies that empower the individual human being. To me all religions are the same at their core and it is necessary for each human being to make her own discoveries concerning the bridge between herself and God (or what we like to call the inner source of life). Every religion, or belief system, seems to adjust to its surrounding culture, and people who crave power put themselves between the individual and their inner source.

No wonder that the most powerful part of spirituality has been hidden from the main part of society. Just imagine if people stopped obeying and became independent of different earthly power systems. What would happen to authorities that claim that they hold the uttermost truth? What would happen to businesses that are based on peoples' fears? Do we need those businesses that make money by "comforting" people so that they for a moment might forget about their troubles?

In the old days the power systems operated openly; like the inquisition of the Catholic Church that killed especially women who had gained spiritual power. Today, it mostly happens in a more sophisticated way. What if my private notebooks fell into the hands of colleagues, officials and managers, who might have a totally different way of looking on life than mine? How can a sane woman believe that her soul has lived many lives, that she is a bridge to spirits existing in other dimensions and that she, through a kind of energy exchange, is concretely creating what the old Egyptian mystery school called "Ka" meaning "the light body"?

In Scandinavia, we are taught to be liberal when it comes to different cultures and religions. However, when it comes to these kinds of belief systems, suddenly something else happens. "This is not science!" is one reaction. "She has become fuzzy!" is another. These are different ways how to neutralise this powerful wisdom as I see things.

Today, sitting at my terrace, I am influenced by what I imagine would be the reactions of people if they found my private notebooks. I even thought of making a warning note, so that the text would not be misunderstood. For a moment I was about to destroy what has been the greatest gift in my life, just because I was afraid of being misunderstood and looked on as crazy.

I'd brought all my books to Mallorca to find a way how to deal with the wisdom I received which had been written in a very spontaneous and personal way. There are some parts that will forever stay just in my own heart, while most of it is shared through this book.

A strong energy wave told me that it was time for a new session of learning. I held my "light hands" as I had been told above my head, fingers lightly together and my thumbs pointing to my head. I felt a transmission of energy moving down my spine. My hands moved to my heart and I received love.

I was shown, in an inner vision like watching a movie, how my whole life has been guided for the last five years in a very specific and concrete way. Or maybe I should say that it was from my part in a more conscious way during these last five years.

This inner session started with me giving thanks for all guidance I have received. I met my fears of being misunderstood and ridiculed. I saw an inner picture of those who might find my books after my death and I saw flashes from earlier lives, when it was life threatening to reveal your spiritual life, especially as a woman. I remembered and heard again: *"Maybe your fears were the excess weight - not your books!"* I began crying still and softly. What was I doing with this great gift, which has been the most valuable in my whole life and has brought the very meaning to my life? Yes, there is a natural scepticism when it comes to things beyond what we are used to seeing and hearing with our senses. I myself have needed lots of support to be able to believe in all the signs that I was shown. This has been my path to "The Power of Trust!" as I named my 2008 business book about leadership.

*"Your inner journey is brilliant and beautiful and is not supposed to be destroyed or hidden!"* I was told by this inner voice.

Finally, my whole body was relaxed. I stayed in my bed for a long time and I cried from liberation and joy. So wonderful to be able to honour my inner journey and also to honour my guide! He did not wish me to hide - quite the contrary!

During the first steps of my inner journey, my guide had to be truly persistent. I look at my notes: *"We need to connect with you without disturbance. It is like a radio transmission. You need to make yourself available without disturbance more often. That is why we knock at four in the morning. Get up, meditate, receive and write it down! You will get strength and power from it. The time has come. Nothing to wait for! It will flow like a stream through you. Meet us there!"*

"Yes, thank you", was my answer.

*"Don´t underestimate yourself! Think big! You can do it, don't ask for it - do it!"* And the voice continued: *"You are creating a bridge*

*between worlds and dimensions. And it is about intuitive leadership in a new era."*

I see from my notes that I had started to write again after a break of more than half a year. In my notebook was a summary of how much had happened through my inner guidance during this time. I had also been extremely busy creating a new company, in combination with my difficult home situation with Mikael´s cancer.

During this intense time, I was guided concretely and daily and my guide was like a colleague on the other side, giving me perspectives that made the whole thing possible. I was assisted by the clairvoyant lady, Doris, who saw my guide clearly and brought messages further to me, again and again confirming that what I myself experienced also independently came to her. My critical mind needed this kind of confirmation.

While reading my notes, I remember those days when I was given signs several times a day. At that time I still needed those confirmations to stay and keep building the bridge. One winter day in Stockholm when walking in the street on my way to my office, I suddenly stopped. Something was happening. To my great surprise, I experienced a triangle in my mind, coming from my guide, falling down to me approaching my heart, where it met another triangle which had its base there and was pointing upwards. Together they made a star. Later I read about this kind of star, but before this moment I knew nothing about it as an esoteric symbol.

There was great joy and thankfulness expressed in my notes. Just a few days before I had received an extra strong message in my daily meditation. Again, my guide put the "leather briefcase" beside me and I got the whole plan, how to bring about and write my business book "The Power of Trust". I was extremely thankful and perceived my coming steps as much easier. I said to my guide: "Yes, we are doing this together. You are among us here on earth." The time of wonder had not passed. I was woken up at four in the morning, the same time as the night before, to receive energies. Every cell received moment by moment. Time stood still. My whole body was trembling; there was heat all the way down my spine from the top to the bottom and from bottom to top simultaneously.

I remember having tickling in both hands, especially in my right hand, which was giving out heat and healing. In this way I am able to heal myself, feel the healing power, and I am able to contribute to the healing of others that are physically close and also to those at a distance. "Stand up for it, this is not me," I told myself. It is a power of love coming through me.

Then a voice started to speak and told me how my life was planned from the beginning. I was shown earlier lives, especially during the time, when Jesus Christ lived on Earth. My guide was there too in that lifetime. We stood together experiencing how tough it was for us human beings to receive love, as love often turned to hate.

I was told what my plan in this life was about - to understand the essence of love. I was shown the difference between universal love and passion based on sex and earthly love between a man and a woman with all its limitations. I was shown the meaning of certain obstacles in my life, and I learnt that love is not about guilt or the sacrifice of my own life.

Through receiving unconditional love from inside and giving it further to others, I was able to receive the message the following summer that Mikael had to face another period of treating cancer. This unconditional love also made me stronger in society and in my work. *Tell thy truth!* came back to me. I read in the book "Presence" by Peter Senge: "There is a becoming future depending on us."

One morning I wake up early; the sun is coming in slowly and gently. My body is full of energies flowing through the bridge between heaven and earth within me. It is difficult to write, the tickles in my right hand are intense and I put this hand in my left. At the same moment an intense beam of light is coming to my head from above, or rather diagonally from above from the right side. It is like a kind of confirming inner ceremony to say that when I am being faithful in making myself available to this inner connection, the bridge is there.

I experienced this as a pillar of light above my head which met a similar kind of pillar from my guide, as it was shown in the great wisdom of ancient Egypt. I learnt that life and death is not the main focus. The focus is how to connect to love and life, while living your life on Earth.

Those were the first steps of building the bridge. Step by step the bridge has become stronger. Today one of my inner sessions was about creating a connection all the way from my three lower chakras and the energy I received from what I call the "androgyne"- a place in another dimension where my higher self and the higher self of my inner guide are linked and balanced. I was shown energy points in my body that deepened the connections and my body turned into some spontaneous yoga movements. The energies met in a kind of creative void, where something new was created. That moment my stomach grew from the energies coming in through my navel. This session continued for a couple of hours, deeper and deeper, until I was ready to surrender from my lowest chakra to the highest. I was totally filled with light energy.

Then the voice came again: *"You wished to be a vessel – this is how you become one. You are supposed to become a pillar of light from the centre of Earth all the way to us. Then we are able to send light without obstacles and know that it will reach the Earth. You are one of many on Earth who functions like this. They are all the little lights on the planet that you have seen in your inner vision."*

This intense day was not yet coming to an end. Later there was another session. I kept the focus in my forehead and my head, as I had been trained to do, and let my physical body release the old tensions of darkness, fears and control. It was all done in a soft and gentle way.

Later that night I was sitting at my terrace, my body extremely soft and tender. I was full of wonder looking out into the harbour, the stars and the sky. The next day I had my appointment with Juan Carlos to continue my body work and I was also meeting my friend and colleague Johannes in Palma.

4.

# Being introduced to my spiritual family

It is early morning and still dark outside. I enjoy the cool air coming in through my open terrace door. There are light clouds and a single star here and there in the sky.

Later today I will go by the local bus to Palma, and this is more than enough of outer discovery and journeying for one day as I am travelling in so many other ways as well. The feelings in my body today remind me of the intense day yesterday. My back is warm and soft. The energies are flowing within me in a soft and gentle way and my skin is extremely sensitive too. It is truly the feeling of being a transformer of energies.

My light hands move to my cheeks and face and to the back side of my neck, slowly and gently. Those are the places that hold a lifelong pattern of keeping things together and taking too much responsibility, so that families, groups and organisations in my old world of thinking would not fall apart. These very old tensions are now being released.

Again I bring my fingers together over my head, my thumbs pointing down. This is to me the place of the androgyne.

The answer is coming directly as waves through my whole body. A voice says: *"We are the ones working with your physical body. "We" meaning the androgyne in another dimension. We are assisting your physical body so that it will be able to receive the high energies that need to go through it, when you are an instrument in the physical world. At the same time we are creating and building the light body, which you will need in order to travel within space and time. All this is done to fulfil our part of the divine plan. This is the fundament and the purpose. Everything else will follow. You are in several dimensions simultaneously."*

My feeling receiving this message is one of calm and deep thankfulness. I come to a deeper understanding and I gain tools. I feel the shift towards a greater spiritual responsibility and an even greater joy.

Now the daylight is lighting up the sky outside my window. So beautiful! I enjoy a lovely breakfast at my terrace slowly preparing myself to go to Palma.

To be outside my little nest is quite special. However, I am in good hands. At lunch with my old friend Johannes we both shared our present life situations and our concerns for what is happening in the world today. I have met many physicians during my long working life, but I have never met anyone like Johannes. To me he is a kind of prototype for medical science in the coming years; he is a pioneer trained in both traditional medicine and integrative medicine, and he is a true bridge builder.

To meet Juan Carlos is literally to be in good hands. His way of working, based on advanced Feldenkreis methodology, is very close to what I have learnt from my inner journeying using light hands as tools. Now my body receives further teachings, deepening the work that started from within.

I have a third appointment in Palma, to go into the huge cathedral. But as I am more sensitive than ever, I cannot stay inside it. For some reason I do not feel at ease and I step outside listening to the impulses where to go and I find my temple at the pond just to the right of the cathedral. There are two swans swimming together in the pond and it's as if they are cleaning the water.

The water flows further into a very special park where many fountains create a specific pattern. At the end of the park, situated next to the swans is a statue called Ionica. She is to me like pure female energy receiving the cleaned water from the swans, then pouring the water further – this life enhancing force - to a long row of twelve fountains on two parallel lines that in the other end finally meet each other at another big fountain facing Ionica. This fountain is to me her male counterpart. Together they create this very beautiful environment. Above the fountains is a roof of trees giving shelter from the burning sun. There are many people coming to this park to just have a break, to sit there and enjoy themselves.

Close to this park, behind the male counterpart is another place that used to be a theatre. Today, as a sign of creativity, a musician is playing caressing flute music. This park is to me a symbol of universal male and female energies, the foundation of creation. I decide to come back and learn more about this special park, a cathedral truly alive. Today I have understood so much more about the meaning of inner guidance. I have learnt about the difference between universal male and female energies in relation to, and separated from, the earthly ones. I feel such a release.

There have been times during my inner journey when I have been confused and I have had difficulties integrating everything into my daily life. Now I understand that I have been trained to be able to distinguish between different kinds of love. There have been moments when I have almost felt unfaithful to my husband, only to later on realise that I had experienced a universal kind of female love energy meeting a universal kind of male love energy. It has been necessary for me to be able to fully surrender to what is called the "inner marriage between the poles," and by doing so finding my inner balance.

Spiritual energy is also about transforming sexual energy into higher frequencies. Love is a creation taking many forms. What has happened within me brings also a kind of deeper love to my husband. Maybe not in the same way as when we were young and full of sexual passion, but today I send him love to all his cells throughout his body.

I realise that I came to a point of no return a couple of years after my inner journey started. When the energies were coming to me, I had to meet them or I would be hit by them. I learnt the clear signs when I did not receive the energies as intended: extreme fatigue, an aching or freezing body. Coming home from work I often just had to take a shower and then rest in bed for a while to later be able to enjoy a nice evening.

I learned to accept that the old structures were falling apart and that I had to say goodbye to previous working environments. I learnt to stay in the *now*, be attentive to impulses, try them out and discern between them. All the way I was directed closely by my guide. It was like having two jobs. On the physical plane I was the chairwoman of the board of a growing company, on the inner plane I was like a managing director with my guide as chairman.

Leaving old structures also meant learning how to take care of my physical body. Finally I understood what I have read so many times: *"Your physical body is your temple, you yourself are God in this temple."* Now it was natural to put myself on a diet to clean my liver and eat more healthy food. My cells were happy and old anger came out. My solar plexus came alive.

My guide and I always made contact through the antennas that I was introduced to during the summer. Very efficient!

At the end of the autumn I felt as if my guide was not as close as before. Through Doris I heard my guide telling me: *"You do not need* **me** *so much any longer, but you will need my energy."* Yes, I had practiced and I was able to stay in contact without the need for these daily concrete moments of guidance.

I recall sitting in my meditation room the following New Year's Day listening to a special meditation called "The Master on the Beach". This is the very special occasion when I first met a Master called Kuthumi. It was a brief meeting and I just heard him say: *"DO NOT DOUBT!!"* This was the starting point to another kind of guidance which was not as close as my guide. It felt like coming home to a place where I wished to learn more about the mysteries of life. Again things just happen. I had never heard of Master Kuthumi, or the other masters, by name until that moment. Just a couple of weeks before, two special books seemed to drop off the shelf in the bookshop I usually go to. I had not seen them there before or after. Later I ordered copies of them. Both books claimed to have been written by Kuthumi. Be that true or not, I learnt more from these books than ever before, so they were meant to come into my hands there and then.

During the same period I had made a booking to go to Mallorca in the early spring to be on my own and to write my business book. I wanted to share with the world the astonishing stories and conclusions from the interviews I'd conducted with twelve selected senior business managers.

I felt certain about the connection between my decision to go, and my introduction to Master Kuthumi. When I make myself truly available for long enough, then I get the answers that I have been longing for. So from that moment I experienced guidance from two different energies and that lasted for a period of almost one and a half years. When this period ended, my guide stopped coming to me in a personal way and my guidance continued in other ways. My experience was however that everything that happened was clearly a part of the School of Kuthumi.

Late in the evening being back from Palma to my apartment after a full day out, I really feel like coming home. It has been a very special day. There is now a nice balance, a mixture of time for my inner journeying and writing, and time with friends and colleagues to explore parts of Palma. It is a warm and calm night and I see the lights over the harbour and hear music from far away. As a woman from a northern country I find it hard to go to bed at a night like this, I feel caressed just sitting here.

# 5.

# Teachings from my cosmic home

I am sitting at my terrace at ten in the morning. The sun is not yet shining strongly, still it is hot. I slept long today, and woke up from a dream. In my dream I saw my husband Mikael walking along the street here in Mallorca, looking into my mailbox as he passed it on his way to the apartment door. He rang the bell. I was happy that he was here. I was happy to be happy and I woke up. I think the dream was influenced by our talk on the phone last night. He told me very clearly that he missed me being around at home. Not that he felt lonely, only that he missed me. Those words were not easy for him to say and I was deeply touched. I do not think that my answer showed him enough how happy I was. We were both a bit shy.

Somehow, my dream made even clearer to me the difference between being in the spiritual world and living here in the earthly world. From my inner source I am privileged to receive unconditional love. And finally I dare receive it. Here on earth, few people are able to either give or receive unconditional love. As human beings we all have our protective layers.

When reflecting on this I recall what happened during my visit in Mallorca a couple of years back. That trip became a turning point in my inner journeying. It became then crystal clear to me that I had chosen my path and I had been brought to a kind of spiritual school in another dimension.

Coming home from that journey, which was both an inner as well as an outer journey, was very tough for both Mikael and me. I had been talking to him on the phone the evening before going back and all was well then. When I came home I found him ill, close to death with thrombosis in his only lung. So we went to hospital and he was taken into intensive care for a week.

There was turmoil inside of me. How could I integrate what I had experienced so intensely in my inner journeying into my daily, practical life?

After a couple of weeks, I was able to live in both worlds again. I realised that my confusion was totally my own. My inner source gave me nourishment and support. I was the one who mixed things up and felt guilty.

Again – what is love about? To live and let live, I understood at an even more profound level. By receiving from my inner source, I was instead able to let this love flow further to my husband.

The time I spent in the mountains of Mallorca on my first trip became to me a point of no return. I was invited to inner sessions day and night. I was also taken to a place where it was up to me to decide to go on or not. In one of these sessions I wake up from the sun coming through the window. Fresh air continues to caress my body as it has been doing gently throughout the night. My body is moving spontaneously and it looks like a kind of yoga movements initiated from within. I am not trained in yoga, but this feels natural to me.

I looked at my alarm clock before starting my morning rituals and realised that I was late and needed to postpone my meditation until after breakfast. I spent the usual time in the bathroom. Then there was a strange gap in time. When I came out from the bathroom it was like someone had changed the hands on the clock. Confused, I realised that I had time for a short meditation before breakfast. The voice came to me saying: *"You have experienced a moment when time is still. Listen to the birds and other sounds around you, see the landscape, and go deeper into it. We will meet you there. This is where the gap in time is, eternity. You can always go there, when you wish. Learn how to! This is how it is happening, the new. You are always welcome!"*

I bowed in thankfulness and respect. The voice came back: *"You don´t have to bow that deep! We are your friends along the path. We have walked before you and we show you the way. In the same way you are showing a way to others on Earth, the torch you speak of. In the same way as you appreciate respect and joy when you assist others, we appreciate this from you. We need your physical hands and feet as part of our plan to assist humankind on its way. That is why we need to cooperate. You do your part – we do our part."*

*"We are in the beginning of a new phase now, you feel it already. You have been cleansing yourself in a good way so far, so that you are able to receive our guidance. Yes, you met Master K on the beach and you saw the white building. We are many here together with him. Your friend, your spiritual brother, is here amongst us, he is greeting."*

*"Your guide and you have had a special assignment through many lives. You and your husband have another kind of agreement – to protect one another. Quite a lot for one lifetime!"*

*"You can only see some parts about the now and the future from where you are at the moment and it is not possible to tell more concretely right now. Keep contact with us, receive from our energies, listen carefully to different impulses and let the web be woven."*

*"The business book you are writing is in line with this. It is in the book possible to express certain things that need to come out in this time. We give you impulses – you express and work them through. We are with you."*

*"Don´t dwell in this now – go and have your breakfast, write afterwards!"*

As I received the message and went on my way, I realised that I was just in time for breakfast. I am taken care of even when it comes to simple concrete details.

Later in the evening I am sitting outside and it is hot. The full moon is glowing. I hear the sheep and I see the lights from the valley while I sit on the terrace on the mountain. What a day! It continued after breakfast. I was through inner guidance healed from a kind of scoliosis that I had had since I was a child. There were fire-like energies coming through to help my body release the old tension. Inner pictures came together with my bodily experience, explaining old family patterns. *"Actually you took on your father´s scoliosis that he got from a disease he had as a child. You wanted already as a little child to "fix" him - out of love of course."*

In my meditation I get very clear instructions from my inner voice: *"You see, you fly with your forehead!"* Aha, I understand, it is when I keep focusing in my forehead that I am able to let go of the heaviness in my body. How beautiful! I continue flying and I arrive at the white building that I had been showed on New Year's Day when I was first introduced to Master K. The voice continues guiding me: *"Look around – dare to ask!"* I arrive in a garden via beautiful roses and I experience endless peace and beauty.

*"You see, we are all gathered here in the etheric realm. We all have our mission. There are many such retreats all around the universe."*

A pattern of eternity and wisdom beyond all human intellect is emerging.

*"It is about frequencies, frequencies of light and sound. When you open yourself to higher frequencies, you are able to experience and sense a beauty so great that it would be impossible to receive on Earth."*

*"We are here, Master K is here, your guide and friend is here. Do you wish to meet him?"*

At a distance I see two beings in white clothes. I have a feeling of the power in their eyes, so I dare not yet look directly, I look from the side. Then a big warm wave of love energy is coming to me. It is filling my chest totally. I can only receive; tears coming from joy.

Slowly, slowly I am leaving this time and place. I am flying via the nature around me, the birds, the sun and the trees before returning to my little terrace.

I also realise that from now on I cannot speak freely about what I am experiencing. I first need to integrate it. However, giving the torch to others and letting this guidance come out into practical action here on Earth - that sounds like music and I am delighted!

I have a few chapters remaining in the book "The Lost Symbol" by Dan Brown. To me the lost symbol is *love*. I wonder what the lost symbol will be to the author?

A warm, calm energy is flowing within me, releasing and receiving. It comes intensely from the androgyne, telling, confirming, giving to me while I am here in my physical body. To receive these energies causes me warm tears of joy.

Again the voice: *"You need to gain perspective yourself of your inner journey before you are able to write about it!"* Of course, how natural! And it is all about my inner process within many dimensions.

On a *bodily level* I realise the close connection between my pelvis, my jaws and my upper thighs. When I let in the light energy from above, old tensions are released. My light hands have the knowledge where to go and they give their light touch far beyond my intellect. They surprise me again and again.

On a *psychological level* I am told that my survival patterns get in the way of me daring to receive on a profound level, especially as a woman in relation to the men I have met in my life.

My path to experience female and male *universal* energies in an extremely loving way has therefore been necessary for my growth on a *spiritual level*. Maybe that goes for everyone? This was for me the key to surrender in order to become a vessel of creation.

What do I mean by being a "vessel of creation"? Master K said to me long ago: *"All portals are sealed, hidden in your physical body. They are lightened up, energised, when they get in contact with the light or sources of higher frequencies. We become our own creators when we learn how to receive and give love – universal love."*

We learn this by lighting up the portals in our own bodies. This can be done in many ways. It is about raising our frequencies and also releasing the old patterns blocking the way.

Heaven encounters earth - from this our consciousness expands. There is nothing as provocative as love, I would say.

A couple of years ago an important book "happened" to come into my hands. I am forever thankful to the two authors, Tom Kenyon and Judy Sion, for their honest and profound sharing of experience and wisdom. The book was called "The Magdalene Manuscript". Tom Kenyon speaks about *alchemy* as a creative transforming process. He says that you need the following ingredients for it to happen:

- *A substance* to be transformed
- *A container* to hold the alchemical reaction
- *Energy* to make it happen

Translated into spiritual transformation it would be, as he says:

- *My light body*
- *My awareness*
- *Kundalini energy*

When reading the books "Hathors" and "Magdalene Manuscript" by Tom Kenyon, I was able to recognise what I had received through my inner guidance. To me it was a relief that others share similar experiences, not only in modern times, but from wisdom several thousand years back in different cultures. I needed the contact with other travellers on their spiritual path, because in my physical world I felt that I was at that time not able to share my inner journey with anyone.

From my terrace I see the boats in the harbour. The sun is setting and it is making the boats shine white from its light. I will soon go for a walk to the little light house to enjoy the sunset over the sea. My body is still fresh from the swim I took during the afternoon.

I am now able to read about this part of my inner journey - the marriage between the poles. I read with a new perspective and I thank my guides, including my own higher self, for showing me the path. I also understand why I had to go to Mallorca this time, to release the part of my body that was stuck from old energies. It would otherwise be a blockage in the creation of my light body. To become a vessel of creation is urgent to me as I need to be in this state to be able to contribute in the way I wish contribute. We are all needed to build a world of harmony and peace. I understand that this profound experience and knowing on many levels is the basis for creating organisations in the new era. I will be able to create organisations together with others sharing this knowledge and I will be able to teach leaders about conscious creation, bringing the essence into practical tools.

The next morning, the sunshine is brilliant, but I am stuck. The evening before I had prepared several emails with the intention to send them all during office time. In this moment I realise that it is not possible to connect. OK, I think, I will have my breakfast, and I read one of my many books on spirituality instead of sending emails. Now, after just one chapter, the energies are taking over and I just have to put the book away and make myself available. I feel the soft loving energy pouring into me through all my chakras. I get filled and I feel happy. Spontaneously I raise my arms above my head.

This is the movement I was told to use last summer and the instructions came from a voice that was also saying: *"The armpits…don't forget the armpits - they are like antennas for us."* I still remember how surprised I was. My intellect would never have been able to come up with such an idea.

Even higher frequencies of energy come into me, and I get an impulse to bring my fingers lightly together above my head over the crown chakra as I have been taught. The androgyne is greeting me: *"Don´t forget what Mother Mary told you; you have the right to be beautiful, radiant and divine. You yourself have now enough first hand experiences. Don´t get stuck reading about others as you have been doing for so many years. The time is NOW! Tell, go out in the world!"*

*"Your idea, that you threw away the other day, of telling about your journey and your experiences from the worlds within worlds, is excellent. It will be exciting for the reader to travel with you on your journey. They will learn more from that than from your conclusions.*

I become excited and happy. I see as an inner picture, how it is possible to be at many places, times and dimensions simultaneously, as this is I in fact how I do experience life. So here I am in the very moment of creating a new book. I knew when I decided to go, but I did not know how.

I recall the process of writing my business book. Then I was closely guided by my guide, my spiritual brother on the other side. I took the result of the twelve interviews with me to Binibona, Mallorca to pull it all together. What I could not predict then was how those days, above all, opened me up for profound guidance and introduced me to my next step on my spiritual path. The veils between the worlds were so thin that I clearly felt the presence of both my guide and Master K.

From then on I experienced within me a true covenant. I knew my cosmic home and I understood that there was a clear purpose behind it all. From that time on, my joy, meaning of life and responsibility as a human being has its source within my cosmic home. This does not make my daily life less meaningful and less happy. On the contrary, it is like the unconditional love from my cosmic home is pouring through my body further to others. I feel more free and happier than ever. To live and let live is so much easier now.

During the many sessions the voice kept asking me: *"Do you now understand why?"* Finally, I do!

One sparkling evening, I had just finished writing the first part of the business book with a prologue thanking my spiritual brother in words suited to the outer world. I had also made a front page helping me in the visualisation of the emerging business book. I went to have dinner in the hotel's little dining room with a book as company as I felt odd dining alone. Suddenly I heard a clear voice: *"Lay down that book, listen instead!"* I felt the presence of my spiritual brother and guide as clearly as if he were there in flesh and blood. I was shivering throughout my whole body and I felt embarrassed being with other people in that state. *"You have to get used to this!"* I heard the voice again coming from my right side. At another table I saw a young man looking at me in a special way. I felt that he was able to see auras and that he was a witness to what was happening. The voice came again from my right side: *"There will be a lot of travelling with this book. The book is a vehicle to get the message out. We are linked together in doing this."*

I managed to stay put, playing the guest-just-having-a-dinner role. I more or less rushed to my room when dinner was over. "What is this?" I thought. *"You have to get used to this!"* I heard again. Then I got a peaceful, personal explanation of how this co-operation will happen, me in a physical body on earth and him on the other side bringing higher frequencies and wider perspectives. It was now the third time the voice had said: *"You have to get used to this!"* This time my answer came from all of me, clear and determined. "Yes!!!" My intention was clear, and I knew that I would be cared for if my fear would come back. *"Your heart chakra is wide as a crater,"* the voice said to me and left for that time.

The day after I am sitting in my room with the view over the valley. I try to understand the pattern of all the sessions I have received from the other side. The inner teachings have been extremely concrete and systematic; do this and do that. They were also combined with perspectives of why so. I always received comments with a friendly humour, especially when I was stuck. There was a lightness and joy in the communication that took away fear, doubt, shame and self-importance.

I feel like a younger sister on my spiritual path, guided by those who have travelled before me. I am being guided with tenderness, joy and humour. I understand now that time is urgent and that I need to be clear about my own "yes" or "no" along this path.

I also understand that this inner teaching is a fruit of my own pure longing and decree. We are many who share a common need and longing to spread the message further to humanity through the flow of co-creation. There are many all over this planet and beyond who are joining with the purpose to spread love and faith bringing harmony to Planet Earth.

*"What is it that is so strange about openings in your bodies? You on Earth have so many ideas."* This was the voice of Master K and his words were the introduction of a session, where I was shown all openings, including the chakras. I was a bit uptight but Master K joked with me in a friendly way. *"You let energy in through your forehead, keep your focus there and then bring the energy to your navel. Let it come into your navel and then bring it out into your whole body. This is where you got your first nourishment as a baby through the navel-string. We can live on prana, which we let in through the navel."* I was shown the openings of the nostrils, my mouth and throat. An old memory from another life time was provoked. *"Here you have a lot of blockages. You have been chained in many lives."* I was released. The voice confirmed that my heart chakra was wide open and continued to show me the solar plexus and the sacral chakra: *"Do it in the same way. Let the higher energy in with your forehead, receive and link it together with the other opening you are focusing on, still keeping the focus in your forehead. Bring it together!"*

My body felt young, vital and filled with joy and I understood in a new way how things are linked together. I felt reborn. *"All openings exist in all seven bodies and they connect and create a whole when we open ourselves to it."* In this way Master K ended this session.

I also remember the day when I decided to go for a walk to another village in the mountains. When leaving the hotel I felt two warm light hands on my shoulders. I opened myself even more and I was filled again and again with loving energy. I walked for a couple of hours and arrived at the village, surprised how heavy I felt the energy there to be. The people I met did not look happy. I bought myself a cup of tea at a café and then walked back.

On my return I went through a beautiful and rich landscape between mountains. I was a bit worried that I wouldn't make it before darkness, but I kept on walking knowing that sunset would keep me company on my way back to the hotel. The voice came to me: "*You choose and you choose from your heart. You felt the same contrast between frequencies as we do when we wish to get in contact with you on Earth. If you don´t raise your frequencies, then it is only possible for us to meet you in short glimpses. There is nothing wrong with that, everyone has their own path to walk. You feel now that you have returned to a higher frequency when you are outside that village. We will be with you and look after you, so that you can make it. You will be filled with new energy.*" This time the energy accompanying the voice was sharper and stronger. I received, I was vitalised, I was happy about my soft body and felt my breathing in a new nice rhythm, a bit faster now. I was in the flow enjoying the nature, the view, the sheep - everything!

Without looking at my watch I made my way home at about half the time as going to the village. I was sweating, still enjoying the rhythm of walking all the way up the hill to the hotel. The darkness came as I passed the entrance to my hotel. After a warm shower I enjoyed a nice dinner.

A couple of days later, after my session about openings, I went for a walk again, now to another village. From the start I got clear instructions on *how* to walk, how to keep the flow while walking. This was a very sensual, alive and non-tiring experience; I did not even feel tired walking up the hills.

I was enchanted by the feeling of being in this village. The energies were so much lighter than in the village I went to the other day. The people looked lighter and I felt at ease there. Life went on and the people did not let themselves be disturbed by a tourist like me. I walked through the village and saw a sign to Llux, the monastery. I felt a connection, I would have liked to own a little house here but it would have been too expensive. However, I send my vision to a future possibility that might just have another form.

Here at my terrace some years later I realise how much I have learnt since those first steps of teaching. This evening the moon is full; soft music is coming from the other side of the harbour. It is very nice and I am thinking back on an intense and creative day. This book is in the shivering moment of creation. I visualise its form and feel excited. I come to the conclusion that I would happily spend the rest of the autumn writing. However, nowadays I trust the process. Besides the need to provide for my daily living, there might be other things for me to understand before I am able to write all the chapters. It seems to be a process within a process within a process.

Today I also fully understand how urgent it was that I was able to understand the message and take full responsibility for my part of the co-creation. My first responsibility is to face my own blockages that are in the way of the flow. It is after having transformed my blocks that I can use my arms, legs, talents, experiences and intent to actually do the practical work. I need to stay available so that these higher frequencies and perspectives can come through to guide me. It is up to me to say yes or no. Then when I have made my vows I have reached the point of no return. There is no way back, only forward.

This path of co creation is a path filled with love, faith and hope. It is also a path with joy and humour. My cosmic home is now the foundation of my life. I know that this has been my inner knowing and longing ever since I was four years old. It is a precious gift. This gift is not only meant for me. I share it with the people around me as we are sisters and brothers along our spiritual paths. This is especially important in this time of great transformations.

My business book was published in late August 2008. It was released at a time when the world economy was peaking. A month later the financial crisis was reality. I wrote in the book: "Love and passion will be the driving forces in the New Era. Today it is a reason for success, tomorrow it will be a necessity." Today I would write: "Yesterday, it was a reason for success, today it is a necessity."

# 6.

# Co-creation between worlds

It is again a very wonderful morning at my terrace. There is a warm sun rising over the harbour. My day started after a very short night sleep just after midnight and I have only slept for a couple of hours since five o'clock. Still, I feel fresh. Last night I listened to a taped session with Marina, an old friend and one of my spiritual teachers. My husband, my youngest son and I joined a journey to the Amazon in Brazil during Christmas and New Year in the mid-nineties when she was working with a project to save the rain forests. The people living there had to be saved first to save the forest. Western civilisation had destroyed their old foundation for living. I had not met Marina since then when I saw an advertisement for a seminar with her in Stockholm and I decided to meet her for an individual session, but not in Stockholm - I decided to visit her where she is living now in the woods north-west of Stockholm. Our session was taped and I now needed to listen to that session again before writing the next chapter. At that time I needed her profound stable bridge to other realms. I had made myself lonely during my inner journey and I needed to share and listen to her perspective. Important things were about to happen and I was concerned not to let old fears interfere. She gave me the support I needed on the way.

"We are on the same wave length" is an expression we sometimes use, maybe often without really reflecting on what it means. To me this old saying has gained a deeper meaning after my inner journeying. Just as I experienced different frequencies in those two villages in the mountains a couple of years ago, we all experience love and joy on another energy level than fear and hate. They are on different frequencies!

During the last five years I have systematically been trained to be able to receive energies of higher and higher frequencies. It is of course a great pleasure to receive so much unconditional love. The other side of the coin is that all old blockages come up to the surface in order to be healed. There is no escape. The passages are really tough but there is also a great release when the blockage is dissolved. That is why my own vows of yes or no have been so important.

It is like saying - yes, this is my true intent and I ask, decree, for assistance, if I get stuck in the passages. Whatever may be provoked in me, there is no going back as that would only hit me like a boomerang.

My "cosmic home" - what do I mean by this expression? To me it means to join your soul friends of similar frequencies. My own experiences tell me that there are large groups of souls that incarnate more or less together again and again. They share a similar purpose like bringing love and wisdom to the earth.

Many people feel drawn to special places, certain people or contexts. I believe that there is something about the wavelength on a spiritual level going on then. I have myself experienced these kinds of cell memories suddenly coming to the surface. To me there is a profound meaning in linking these memories to my present life to heal me and to help me gain new insights and inspiration.

The first few years of my intense inner guidance I experienced the voice I heard coming from my friend and spiritual brother. Today I understand that my own higher self was involved as well, as it always is. It is me in another dimension on a higher frequency beyond fear etc.

When I now look back at our physical lives together, I remember that we used to introduce each other to other people like that - as spiritual brother and sister. People around us found it just as natural as we did. We were not lovers on a man-woman level. We had other tasks together. Instead we often introduced a new partner to each other as you do in a physical family. So already then, we were like a spiritual family and our brother-sisterhood was fundamental to us.

So when I started to get those "knockings" from the other side half a year after his death, I was in one way surprised, but deep inside not. It was like continuing our work. Some of my friends were concerned that I had not be able to say good-bye. To me it was different; it was like a task that needed to be completed. As I have said before, I was then introduced to Master K and what I call my cosmic home. All the concrete and loving teaching sessions that I had received were in my experience coming from this ethereal school. This is in essence why I am so extremely grateful for my inner guidance. When heaven and earth truly meet, something new is created on many levels and in many dimensions. This divine co-creation is expressed in many different ways, like in arts, science, building of new organisations etc.

We human beings are both animals with instincts and spiritual beings capable of being intuitive and creative. It is up to each and every one of us to make that bridge. When we bring groups together, where each individual has the capability to bridge the worlds, then the power will be not the sum of the people in the group, but the result will be exponential. In a group of seven, the power will be seven times seven, seven times. You can just imagine what can be accomplished in such constellations!

Our planet today is in desperate need for healing and creative, constructive projects. I am sure that we need the inspiration and guidance from the other side to be able to raise our frequencies to give us wider perspectives. They in turn need our hands and feet, talents and experiences linked with our true intent and love.

I remember one time at our summer cottage by the sea. It was midsummer evening. My body obviously wanted to tell me something. Again I was in a situation of taking on too much responsibility. This pattern has been a common theme in my life. I learnt this pattern very, very early and let my right hip carry too much. I recall the intense energy that came to help me loosen the tight muscles and I felt like my hip was searching for a new position. While doing that the pain was very heavy. Very old sadness and fear come out. A combination of heat, some mild pain-relieving pills, and, above all, meditation through my chakras made me finally OK enough to be able to celebrate midsummer evening, an important day in Sweden.

The day after, the pain was there again, but not as bad as before. Again the energy flowing through my chakras is my best healer. I woke up from a sharp beam of energy coming into my head from the right. I felt it to be a sign that an inner session was going to come and so it was. The inner voice was speaking to me: *"Do you now understand? Let your vessel, your pelvis, gather energy from Mother Earth. Let yourself be filled. We bless you, your vessel and its energy. This is needed so that heaven and earth can come together."* I felt joy spreading in my whole body and reflected that this is how the root chakra is linked to earth. I have read about it, but this inner teaching is so much more concrete.

My arms are sensitive and I notice certain points are influencing different chakras. The voice again: *"Your arms are the rest of your wings. You will also be able to fly with them in your energy body. That is why they are now so sensitive as you also noticed in Mallorca this spring."* My heart understood fully, but my intellect had to put these words to rest at that time.

As my lovely summer vacation continued, so did my inner guidance and I was contacted by the other side many times. My hip was healed through their guidance and it found a new position.

I one day got clear directions from Master K and my guide concerning a coming project, a modern variation of a mystery school applied in the new era. The inspiration was from Pythagoras and his unique school in Crotona, Italy. I got directions of who to contact and connect with and when I phoned them they were all online and available, although they usually are very busy and hard to reach.

During the night I woke up at three in the morning in the middle of an inner session about one of my deepest fears. I saw people bullying based on envy and fear and I was their target. I felt like I had experienced this during many life times. At that moment the inner voice said: *"Now it is time to rebalance your right hip, now that you are soft enough there and in the rest of your body."* And I was guided and healed moment by moment. After a couple of hours I was totally calm and I fell asleep again.

Later the voice came back telling me about how different parts of the body are linked together, giving me a kind of a map. What used to be tensions were now turned into heat. We came to the lower part of my breast cage and I remember how my ribs have always bulged. The voice was determined: *"Stay here! You have all kinds of reasons for rushing from this. This is your fear of receiving love, unconditional love. You need to receive here, otherwise you cannot give. This is the place where universal love is given to you from the masters. Put your hand around your right breast and receive. Feel!"* And finally I dared stay in the moment and I experienced a soft, calm breeze of grace coming through all of me, Christ energy. How wonderful - just imagine, I was on my way to run away from all of this!

Later that morning I woke up with an intense energy in my crown and forehead; the energy flowing further into my arms and hands. It happened in a very light way and with a special, new feeling. *"You are receiving the Holy Spirit!"* I heard the voice say. *"This is a power that is allowed and it's only possible to use it to do good. This is why you have needed to cleanse yourself a lot before. Receive and see the dove!"*

*"This is the answer to your decree and your clear intent. Yesterday, you cleansed yourself from being ahead of the process and you surrendered into sleep. This is where we are able to reach you."*

I felt this healing power in my hands and arms. I was thinking of my youngest son going with his friends on a, as I felt, dangerous car ride on the German autobahns. Love was rising within me.

*"You can send shelter and love through the Holy Spirit"*, the voice says. I stretched out my arms as to bless them. I saw all three

before my inner eyes. My whole body was warm and vibrating at the same time as I really felt that I was letting these high energies be sent further. I saw many doves fly to them and there was a pleasant feeling in my arms and hands.

*"Try to move yourself to where they are"*, the voice says. And I travelled with my forehead and "saw" all three of them. I "visited" each of them and gave them love, energy and shelter from the inner source as it was given to me. This experience then changed from giving shelter to specific people into giving this energy to the whole planet Earth. I felt like holding the globe in my arms. The energy I was receiving was so strong that it was a joy to receive and send further. The more I let the energy flow further, the more my body became warm and vibrating.

One winter evening half a year later when I went to bed the energies were so strong that I, as many times before, had to go to our little guest room as I needed my own space. I asked to be brought to my cosmic home, the etheric school, to meet Master K and my spiritual brother. My prayer was answered. I was guided to open my portals. The energy came straight into my neck and found its way through my body. I surrendered and fell asleep like being in invisible arms.

In the morning I woke up as usual a couple of minutes before my alarm clock. During my shower I received a clear message. *"Today you are not supposed to do your morning "gymnastics"* (very soft movements). *Instead meditate and receive energy. Sit where you usually sit and light a candle."*

I did as I was told and soon heard a voice. I asked: "Who are you?" *"I am Kuthumi."* was the answer. *"I will bring you. Remember that all portals are in your own body. Be aware and follow!"*

I followed and I felt an intense heat in my root and sacral chakras spreading into my legs and up the spine. It was a very intense heat and still a universal feeling. Then the heat spread upwards through all the chakras and a strong energy came from above into my crown and forehead. The energies merged within me and dissolved tension in my neck, jaw and solar plexus, especially at the back. There was a new kind of feeling there.

Then I was suddenly at the door leading to a big room that was filled with an intense light. I was asked to come in to this room where there were many light beings. They all had a similar kind of pillar above their head, a pillar of light. Amongst all these beings was also my spiritual brother. *"Welcome home!"* Master K said.

Finally home, was my feeling. All this longing through my whole life! This big room and these light beings is a part of me as well, one of many dimensions within me. How rich and wonderful! Slowly and very carefully I was brought back to this reality and dimension. What I have experienced is still living in me. And my neck is totally changed.

The next day brought a calm and lovely morning. In my meditation I was now consciously going to the big room where I had met all the light beings. I was staying at the threshold asking if I was invited to come in. Suddenly I heard the birds singing intensely from the garden outside and I felt someone present. "Who are you?" I asked. *"Kuthumi."* was the answer. *I want to bring you there via the singing birds. Travel with your forehead as I have told you. Remember that all portals are in your own body. It is about staying focused and following."*

Again we came to the big room and I got some personal blessings and instructions. Then he told me that he especially wished to use me as an instrument for a particular purpose.

*"It is about the young people who are caught in misuse of the internet and TV. They get doped and lose their sensitivity and sense of living. You have seen this closely around you. You don´t have to work directly with this. Use your position, your power and your love. Awaken love in people's hearts!"*

*"Your own suffering around this issue is a part of releasing love and for you to understand. Tell your truth!! Go with your passion! There is a meaning behind this."*

This guidance, and many other moments like this, was a great source of inspiration to me, while the last part of my former book "The Power of Trust" was created.

During Christmas time that year I found myself to be in a unique situation, as I was staying in bed instead of making the family dinner. My youngest son had got the terrible stomach flu that usually spreads in the winter. He had never been as ill before and I had to call an ambulance. But due to infection risk he had to remain at home. We received help and he slowly recovered. My husband was also ill. Our home turned into a quarantine area instead of being a place for family gatherings.

I experienced many dimensions in what happened besides the illness as such. We were as well clearing up old family patterns and I learnt to keep the disease away by staying in the higher frequencies.

There is a kind of unexpected meaning behind everything, I believe. Not that I wished anybody to be ill, of course. However, when that anyhow was a fact, I made Christmas into a private retreat.

When I read my notes from that Christmas, I recall how strong the messages were that I got. They were truly linked to the situation on our planet. I was in the process of writing the last part of my business book and we were on the edge of entering a recession that we did not know about. Master K was very concerned. From the guidance received I wrote the last two chapters in my book.

To me there are great signs of a new era coming. We are all needed to bring in hope, peace and love. We share a common home. Whatever we might do to hurt our neighbour will come back to ourselves as we are all the same. We need to learn how to co-create *with life* instead of against life.

One way for me to contribute and to co-create is to dare speak my truth and not let myself be silenced.

# 7.

# Endless guidance transforming old blockages

The sun is glittering over the water of the harbour. The beauty is endless and calm. My neighbours are having breakfast and it is nice to hear their voices at a pleasant distance.

Inside of me I have asked Mother Mary to help me not to forget who I am on a soul level, my blueprint. I need this female power and love from within, so that I do not get caught in old patterns. This is the birth right for all of us and I am in my right to be "beautiful, divine and radiant". It is strange how we human beings cut off this divine love by making entanglements of different kinds, all due to fear, control and survival strategies.

I was shown the book that you are now holding in your hand and it was ready to be published. I saw a beautiful photo introducing each chapter.

I visited the park in Palma again yesterday and I connected with the statue Ionica, the one that I experience as the universal female, and all the fountains she is sheltering with her body - the water of life. The roof of the park made of leaves gives shadow from the burning sun. There was the pond with the two swans. Yesterday, the water was fresh and clean. Inside of me I gave the swans credit for that, although being in this reality as well I realise that they got some physical human assistance. And why not?

I am now at a point when I can honour and respect the very special inner journey that has been given to me. I wish to make this book beautiful to dignify that. I like the text to be a bridge between people, to those who are into a spiritual culture and to those who are not. I hope to inspire you to feel that you together with everyone else have the potential to be your own creator. This is your birth right and it is needed in this time on Earth.

Maybe I will later be able to share more of the inner mysteries I have experienced along my path but I first need to understand more myself. I have a strong feeling that there will be more openness around these experiences as time passes.

In the afternoon I again have one of the many inner sessions that are there to teach and heal me. After thirty years of all kinds of psychotherapy, I have not yet found anything as efficient as these "light exercises" as my friend Marina calls them. "Keep doing your light exercises," she said, "and everything else will follow." Now the inner voice is saying: *"Remember what you have heard before that your body is your temple. All portals to the deepest wisdom are hidden there."*

*"You are becoming a purer channel. What you yourself are receiving, is poured further out to people around you in your practical life. That is the whole idea of it."*

*"As you have been trained throughout many years in a special way, you are trusted with tasks linked to that. You already know. During five intense years you have learnt how to be your own creator. Now you know!!"*

Now you know! It is true. Now I know. And now it is up to me to take responsibility for who I am and what my task in life is about. My children, my husband, my younger colleagues are all independent. They do their thing here on earth. My task *now* is to stand on my own two feet in the spiritual world on earth.

It is all about love. You need love and faith to be able to surrender and receive. Your own love, hope and longing are what open the door to the other side. The creation happens in that encounter and your aura gets filled with energy.

I once was a participant at a conference arranged by Peter Senge, a leading and famous organisational consultant from the USA. When I had read his book "Presence" for the fourth time, I realised that I wished to go and find out in person what it was I was so happy about. There was a flavour that made me feel at home, a thinking that was similar to the way I do process work in organisations within the Gestalt framework and I was curious about how that was applied in the hearts and heads of more than four hundred people from forty-five countries. I have always been very curious.

There were of course other more private reasons for going. As I went on my own, I made this trip into a retreat. And I did need my own space. All the sessions of "light exercises" also included messages how to create and build, I was on many levels at the same time and in many dimensions. Being a bridge builder is exciting and necessary and it is also tough. The rhythm of going away regularly to have enough space for the creation to happen is what I have found works for me. Otherwise the demands of everyday life might turn into blockages stopping the flow.

My inner voice is speaking to me in the midst of a conference session held in a huge tent: *"You are here for many reasons. One is to get in contact with colleagues around the world and also to give some of them your book.* (I had done a homemade translation of the business book into English for that very reason.) *Don´t hide or underestimate yourself! Speak your truth! You need to do this. Still the main reason is that you are here fully present and get an overview of what is going on around the world concerning projects of different kinds. When you at the same time keep yourself open with me, we are able to connect to concrete projects, contribute and support."*

The journey to the conference turned into a very special experience. I was inspired by some of the Indian colleagues. We share the same way of working with processes in an organisation. However, they have been doing it in huge companies and I wish to learn from them. Both they and I in our organisational work apply some very important common understanding. It is about co-creation and how you first build the matrix with your thoughts and intent. It is then created on an energy level in another dimension. From that matrix certain impulses turn into a pattern that become meaningful to the individual. Then creation on a physical level is taking place.

Back home again after this valuable conference, I received further inner sessions. This morning in my meditation after my soft movements was very special. A strong beam, thin and penetrating, went through my head and made my body open and warm, especially in my root and sacral chakras. I was told to bring my left hand to my right in a special way and press lightly on a certain spot. My brain received energy that moved around, that vitalised and deepened. I experienced a presence on my left side and recognised it as being Master K.

*"This is how we do. Now you know! Keep yourself available regularly and keep yourself open. Not all this trash intervening!* I felt his tender smile while he said that. *You influence others through us. In this way we fill you up directly into your brain, and your whole system raises its frequency and becomes more useful."*

Now the heat from the beam is lightening all the chakras, especially my root and sacral chakras. I understand that I have a lot to learn. The key is to receive and surrender, not for a second to be ahead due to excitement or the need to know.

This beam kept penetrating my head and brain all day through. Yes, I felt I was getting an intense infusion of energy parallel to my ordinary work filled with consultancy, emails and invoices.

Sometime later one day I wake up from a dream. Through the dream I was beginning to understand what it means to be a transmitter, an instrument. I understand with my body where my intellect does not have to understand.

In my dream I was shown high voltage, highly charged electricity, flashes of lightning etc. The name was something like the "high voltage area". This is a field of polarising forces that need to be united and integrated with each other.

It was connected to where the young people are today with their consciousness, and where people like me are. *Trust* is the key for making progress. It is about letting one energy come in and meet the other energy, so that what is to be developed will develop. If we lock ourselves out, nothing will develop.

In the dream there are a lot of forces pulling in different directions. I was demanded to understand, recognise and to invite the high voltage area instead of resisting it. Then development will happen. The image was somewhat like a mathematical equation. It was very natural in my dream and I am thankful that I was shown. I told my dream to my husband Mikael and he immediately understood. To him the high voltage area is like a transformation station. We both agree that young people are not influenced by us older unless there is true contact, authentic contact on an I-thou level.

In my mind the younger generation incarnates with higher frequencies than we did. At the same time they are sort of kidnapped by forces who would like to eat from their energies. Ruthlessly these forces make money from taking advantage of young people's vulnerability by exploiting their needs for clothes, make-up, entertainment leading to misuse of TV and the internet and the use of drugs etc.

I believe that these young ones come in to teach us, the older generation, the widespread insanity in competing for everything. The whole idea of "winners and losers" is draining our life force. What is so wonderful about winning? If someone is winning, another one has to lose. I do not get it.

Other people I believe show us how fundamentalism is destroying and misusing the inner core of religions for their own power purpose. Everything is brought to the surface so that we will need to face it, learn and eventually heal it.

We will be forced to raise our frequencies and meet each other from our hearts beyond all this trash. The dream came to show me this process, I feel. I woke up with a lid before my ears and rather shaky. I also realise that the polarising forces are different parts of me as well. There is homework to be done.

Spring was coming with a warm sun and birds singing. I remember I wanted to make our garden beautiful by planting flowers. While doing this a strong and warm energy is coming from earth meeting a strong, warm energy coming from above and they meet in my heart with joy.

One evening later that spring when I was going to bed an intense beam of light came into my head again. When I make myself available and just receive, I get extremely vitalised and energised. When I do not I get tired. That day I needed to choose. So I asked the beam of energy:

- What do you want!

- *I want contact with you.*

- For what?

- *To focus on what is important.*

- What is important?

- *The bigger perspective, the vision, the networks. Those parts that build further. Give yourself even more time to meditate and receive inner images of what you are supposed to do, your task!*

- How can I do this in the best way?

- *Decree, ask for help, listen and be alert!*

- What does it mean when I hear these little sounds?

- *That you have company, our presence.*

- Please, tell me more!

- *You are now in a new phase, where you are getting energised, charged, to be able to receive even higher energies. You are supposed to transform these energies so that you will be able to contribute to the divine plan. Remember your inner image of all the lights around Planet Earth. You are supposed to plug in there. You are there with your group. Next step is to get a more clear contact with all the other lights covering Planet Earth. Sometimes, you get stuck in details within you and your own group. You have bigger tasks! Your guide, your spiritual brother is often reminding you of that. Don´t forget this!*

- What step will be good for me to take?

- *When you have a second free, you almost become paralysed. That is because we send you extra energy. You get like a gap in time. Instead of getting paralysed then – be alert! Meditate, listen, feel, receive inner images and write, like now! This is what you needed to do this evening, not making invoices. You will have time for that. Learn to make priorities, notice when it happens in a light and natural way and when it happens in a heavy way. You know where to go. Where is your joy?*

– What am I supposed to focus on?

– *Give yourself time and proceed with your book and the network – your two pillars this spring. You need to do other things in daily life, but don´t lose these two parts. They bring you out into the world and above all – they unite you with the other lights on the planet.*

– Where is my spiritual brother now?

– *He is linked to you. You are united and blessed. He is working from his side, uniting the lights around the planet linked to dimensions that you are not yet ready to understand. He is a mentor to you concerning the second ray and Master K. He is happy about what you are doing and he is impatient, he does not understand all the little things you let yourself be occupied with. His perspective is beyond the physical, has always been and now he is not tied. He is happy in his dimension and needs your hands and feet to assist in creating Pythagoras´ school in a modern version.*

– What steps does he see?

– *More and more entrances. They are woven from different directions and will suddenly click together. It will be in different steps but in the year 2016 there will be a clear step. A breakthrough for the earth.*

– *Changes happen like that – sudden "clicks". Lots of threads are swarming and so the network clicks together and a new era has begun.*

– *You are many on earth who are still under the surface of old resisting structures. Don´t go into despair, when you see so much darkness! Everything will come up to the surface.*

– Am I doing the right thing to do this intestinal rinse?

– *You know that already, as you have made the appointment! It will cleanse you, so that you will be an even more sensitive instrument. You will also be more aware of what kind of food you want to bring into your body. Yes, you want to get rid of your extra stomachs and get freer in your body. Use your summer for that, among other things. Decree, pray and receive!*

– Thank you so much for your guidance!

– *You say that often, we feel it and we feel joy. We also thank you for being persistent in opening yourself. Now we just made little noises to make ourselves known to you. Have faith in yourself and continue even further! You have a lot ahead of you! Are you really tired now or is it about taking another step?*

By these words I put my pen down and started travelling with my forehead. Thank you!

When I later on in the evening was resting in my little flat in Puerto de Andratx I heard a voice saying "It is completed!" I had been lying on my bed, very still and calm, receiving and experiencing high energies of great volume and power coming into me from above uniting with my now liberated warm energies in my root chakra, the very end of my spine. I experienced peace and calmness in a way as never before. The energy was of an impersonal, universal kind. This little half hour of rest measured in regular clock time, has for me been like the space of the whole universe in the measure of importance. Again within me I thank my inner guides for being so patient with me along my path. When I read my notes I feel embarrassed for being so caught up in details of my daily life in spite of such strong and persistent guidance. This weakness of mine might be turned into strength, when I finally get myself together as a bridge builder between worlds.

8.

# Learning what love really IS

I am sitting on a bench under the pergola of leaves in the park close to the cathedral enjoying the nice shadow and listen to soft music from a man playing saxophone. In my inner life it is like I am taught about some of the life mysteries of this park. The park is of course what it is for each person as well as for the one who once constructed it. I am curious who this person is and what artist made the sculpture Ionica. We all colour our surroundings with our own experiences and feelings. That is the basis of creativity. As long as we are aware of this, we are free to speak and the exchange will be fruitful. When we start to impose our own way of colouring upon another human being, claiming that my way of colouring is right and yours is wrong - then we get into trouble. This way of acting is what starts wars on earth. I remember a poem I received from my friend Aniesa: *"...beyond right and wrong doing, there is a field – I will meet you there."*This poem is by the famous Sufi mystic Rumi.

I hear my inner voice: *"We – the androgyne - are the swans while you, being on Earth in your physical body, are the statue Íonica. Together we create the water of life that the fountains pour out. We also create the beautiful green leaves living from that water covering the fountains. This is the image of how all functions."*

*"Did you notice that the water is even cleaner today? We are in the same way assisting you to become a more pure channel, so that you in the best way can reach other human beings. Do you see how happy and refreshed they look by just sitting here in this park?"*

*"The female energy is so much needed in this time on earth. You together with many, many others, are helping to create oases around the planet through yourselves."*

*"Remember what you have heard before! Your own body is your temple. All portals to deeper wisdom are sealed in there."*

*"Did you notice that Ionica is not there alone and deserted? She is surrounded by fountains behind her and on both sides. There is a little one just for her, right behind her. So it is! As you by the day become a purer channel, the water that is poured further to other people is more and more clean."*

*"'The Holy Grail is the womb of a woman, your pelvis. Read about it in your book "The Human Aura", in the chapter entitled "The Cradling up of the Mother.""*

How clever to show me this place in Palma, so that I on a deeper level can understand what is happening with me. It is all arranged for the best when it comes to the worlds within worlds.

I come to think of Doris and the importance of her guidance. It has been very much needed through my years of inner journeying. Her independent readings have calmed my own sceptical and critical mind down. For that reason I have told her very little of what was going on inside of me. So when I got her readings, they were genuine and mostly right on the spot. Sometimes I discovered years later how exact they actually were. I am forever deeply thankful to her!

We are a group of people meeting regularly with Doris with the purpose to deepen our intuition. Each time includes a short reading to everyone.

I recall one occasion with Doris and as always my guide is there with us. She sees him and I feel his presence: *"I see a strong and clear water fall in your aura and beside you I see an Indian. Your spiritual brother is introducing him to you. His name is Running Water. Then your spiritual brother looks happy and a bit shrewd about how all these rebuses are coming together, all the threads in the web. He adds that there will be a blooming with focus of stamens and pistils."*

Later that year she said, without knowing anything about my summer: *"There has been a lot of yin-yang for you this summer."*

Besides my intense inner life, a lot was going on in my daily professional life "out there". My business book was to be ready for printing and I was working full time as an organisational consultant building a new company together with my colleagues. No wonder that I had that dream about the high voltage area!

Right after that dream all sorts of technical equipment, our car, my computer, my email connection and parts of electricity at home, started crashing. When this period of time was at its peak, I fell and hit my knee twice. I ended up in the sofa at home crying out: "I need help. I am not good at computers. I need someone to be nice and gentle with me, someone who does the difficult things and someone I can ask. To me it is worth a lot of money to get this. I do not want to focus on this myself!"

As always, when I finally express my need, the help is there. A colleague of mine recommended a special shop in Stockholm, where you get good service. I got the help I needed. When I looked around in the shop, I saw a couple of other ladies of my age, seemingly wishing the same as me. "Is this your special offer, to help older ladies out?" I asked. "Might be, it takes a certain amount of psychology, as well as technique," the man in the shop answered with a twinkle in his eyes.

During the last weeks, before summer holidays that year, the energies were stable and strong all day through as well as throughout the evenings. They made my work very efficient even if I needed to rest now and then. I remember feeling the presence of my guide in a very strong way and my mobile went crazy, almost like it did a few years before. When I gave myself a wonderful moment in the sun then I experienced a wave of energy pressure from above and all the way through me. Then I became calmer and was able to work efficiently again. The night before going to the photographer to take a photo for the business book I found it difficult to sleep. I experienced that we are two going there, but it is only me being visible to the physical world. It is a bit like celebrating, completing the conversation we had at the dinner table in Binibona, Mallorca the year before.

In my car on my way back from midsummer celebrations my mobile was ringing. "Hello, this is Johannes. I am on my way to Stockholm. Are you free to meet on Thursday? I will run a seminar with Justo from Bolivia on Friday and Saturday." "Of course," I said. "I will just check with my family." I prolonged my stay in Stockholm and joined the seminar. It was of course meant to be. It was a seminar exchanging medicine wisdom between Justo, a trained medicine man according to his culture and tradition, and Johannes, trained both in Western medicine and nature medicine. What a bridge that was made!

I asked Justo for an individual session. He works with the flower essence and certain rituals linked to that. So he asked me to bring a flower for the session. In the morning, before leaving home, a bit late with at least one hour to drive, I looked at the beautiful peonies in our garden. They were magenta coloured and they looked as if they were resting on the high green grass. My practical mind took over and I went into the car. After two or three kilometres I realised that I was not able to put these flowers out of my mind. So I had to make a decision. What was more important? To bring this special flower and be a bit late or to be in time? It may sound as an easy decision to make but to me it was not. So I turned the car, went back and took this beautiful flower to the seminar room. Justo arrived after about half an hour, so I had lots of time to give myself peace.

We went outside and he performed some rituals, circles and other things. We communicated with our hands and feet and the few words I knew in Spanish. To begin with I did not feel anything. Then suddenly I started crying and a deep sadness was flowing through my body. Later it turned into joy. Justo was looking at a special direction telling me that someone was approaching me. Later from Johannes´ translation, Justo described that he had seen a light figure coming to me saying: *"Now, you have found your flower!"*

I got further instructions how to drink the flower essence he prepared during the next four days. He also showed me that I need to walk, to use my legs more. What he actually meant by "flower" in this context and in its deeper meaning, is still for me to discover. I just know that there are many dimensions to it.

That summer, universal male and female energies met and merged within me. It all happened on an energy level. Still my physical body was vitalised, so that I felt ten years younger. So much more efficient than all the cosmetics in the whole world to a woman like me being sixty-two years of age!

Today, I know that my guide was what I call the androgyne, meaning my own higher self linked to my guide. At that time I was a bit confused and almost felt a bit untrue to my husband.

However, from what I have been reading in this magnificent book "The Magdalene Manuscript," which I referred to before, there are two paths in what they call the "alchemical union". There is the better known tantric path, where you together with your partner transform sexual energy into higher frequencies and there is the path of Horus, when this happens inside you as an individual being on your own. Then energies from your sacral chakra merge with energies from your upper chakras. So that summer the book was of great help for me in understanding what was happening. Also the book "The Eagle and the Condor" by Jonette Crowley put words to my experience. At that time, I was too shy to tell anyone about my inner world.

I woke during one summer night realising that I was receiving energy into every cell in my body. It was very concrete at a certain point in my neck and at the tail of my spine and all the power and energy flowing between these points was very intense. The voice says: *"We need to always come both from above and below. You needed to fall asleep first, so that it would be possible to reach you, so that you would let us in."*

*"Remember that all the codes are in your own body, the openings, the portals. You are now initiated into a new step. The energies and the happenings will be even faster."*

I experienced an inner question as if I was prepared and ready for the next step and I answered: "Yes" three times. After the merging of energies, I was shown certain points as a kind of map of energies all over my legs and arms. I understood that certain points were linked to different chakras and different kinds of energy. The teaching was done like - if you do this, this will happen etc. So wisely arranged, I thought and wished that I could turn it into a visual map!

*"We are working like this with some of you on Earth, when you are open to it. It is a way to raise the energies on earth and it is urgent. You will understand more later on."*

*"You got that book in your hands, so that you will understand how it works. It is about different kinds of love! Universal love and love on earth.*

Later that summer I got further instructions and experiences. I was shown how I on a universal level was linked through my light hands with my guide and through a place just to the right of my heart to Master K. I understood that these instructions would lead me to an even more intense journey and that I had no idea where it would end. When I think back on this summer, I feel and understand that I have received an invaluable gift. This is all about life force! When we allow the energies between heaven and earth to meet and merge, we become our own creators of life itself. All the energies and all openings in our bodies are wonderful gifts. It is all about how we as human beings think of them, use them or in worst case abuse them. By linking and merging our instincts with higher energies, we create. These creations may be expressed in all kinds of ways.

This, being in a way such an intimate kind of learning, is in essence applicable also within business life. Every time you bring a vision from your true heart with the intent beyond your own desires into action, you are your own creator. The key is to learn about the different states of being, so that you recognise when you come from your true heart.

When I was at the conference in Muscat, and met all these colleagues from all over the world, I was amazed and happy to find that all agreed: "You need to have a vision coming from your heart to be able to create an organisation that will be successful in a sustainable way." To me this was very confirming as I had then just finished my business book. The title of the last chapter is: "Heart and Passion will be the driving forces in the new era." How inspiring to know that many, many around this Planet Earth agree on this! And that there are a lot of lights of hope around the globe believing in love, the fundament for sustainable progress!

9.

# To surrender means total surrender

Today has been a day of rest to integrate the intense session of body work with Juan Carlos yesterday afternoon. He was assisting me in loosening very old tense muscles, especially in my jaw, throat, pelvis and knees. When I went back to my little nest I had to go by taxi. My body was shaking. Still, I was happy to get rid of this old burden. Now, after a day of rest, I am sitting here with the view over the harbour, sun soon approaching the horizon. The beauty is breath taking! Beside me is a box of raspberries - my favourite berries - and half a glass of white wine. This is my first glass of wine besides a glass of champagne at Johannes´ home some days ago. Alcohol does not go well with high energies.

I feel like celebrating both the release of the old burden in my body and also the knowing that this book has found its form. It reminds me of how I a couple of years ago was celebrating my former book together with my spiritual brother and that he was invisible to most people. Then I was really shaky. Today, I have got used to the fact that I am living in more than one world or dimension at the same time.

I have learnt, and can now manage most of the time, to calm down my own critical, fearful mind. I am not only partly, but with all of me, a more humble being – a tiny spot in an enormous universe, or rather universes. Who am I to know all the mysteries sealed in this vast, endless space? Even scientists of today speak about the idea of eleven dimensions within each other.

I believe that there have always been people, who within themselves have been experiencing these dimensions, or they have at least experienced more than our physical, third dimension we share on Earth. Those experiences have been written about independently in different parts of our planet. Eventually, they turned into religions and dogmas and the original experience became like fairy tales. That is why you need to make your own discoveries to find out what is true for you. Spiritual coaching at its best, in my view, is about assisting another human being to discover and listen to her own higher self and inspire her to create an inner dialogue from there with the physical person living here on earth now.

Most of us need this kind of inspiration and awakening to remember who we are in another dimension. Then we also often need some assistance when old blockages come to the surface to be healed. All of us have the divine sparks within us. This also means that we will make our different spiritual journey when, and if, we wish to.

Already when I was thirty years of age I was fascinated by the books written by the journalist Paul Brunton. Out of pure curiosity he travelled systematically to the countries of origin of different religions or belief systems. He wished to understand the kernel and essence of each and every one of them. He found that at the core and in essence they were all the same. You need to go beyond all the dogmas made by the followers of the highly developed spirit who once initiated that specific religion.

In Spain, during the ninth century was an important meeting between Jews, Christians and Muslims. They looked at what they had in common, not what kept them apart, which is often the case. They focussed on the experience of love and peace and the necessity of facing your own shadow before you judge someone. They expressed the mysteries of life in different ways. Still they agreed that there *are* mysteries, meaning that we human beings are not able to have all the answers. Life itself knows more!

When I read my notebook from last summer and autumn I see that I, at that time, was overwhelmed by what I was shown. In my wildest imagination I would never have been able to make up this story. I was myself a true receiver as I was shown parts of the mysteries of life. I understood then and I see it even more clearly today, that there was a certain purpose in this. Through this guidance, I was brought to the very purpose of my life. I experienced that I had agreed to this before I was born. The directions were clear and sometimes tough.

I recall one evening when I fell asleep and then woke up again. A strong energy from above was approaching and I was longing for contact. A voice was saying: *"You are now being prepared on many levels. We send energy directly into you as a transfusion. What you throughout the days are experiencing in your arms and legs, has to do with this. You have asked for it and you get it. You are being prepared for tasks ahead of you that are of a kind that you are not able to imagine now."*

*"One way or another, find ways to translate your business book, so that it will be spread! And you will write more after that. What you can do now is to refine your tools – i.e. yourself and the book. You can also create a web of contacts."*

There was an intense tickling in my right hand as it was receiving a lot of energy as was my whole right arm, especially on the inside. And it was spreading over all the right part of my body. I woke up the day after with a feeling of electricity all over my body. The voice again: *"We give you energy step by step, so that your ´KA-body´ that is your ´light body´ can be developed. This is what your process in essence is about. That is why all steps in this direction are valuable and you don´t need to ponder about as to where this will lead. You are in good hands. Do your part and you will find your path!"*

It felt calm within me. My thoughts wander off too often together with my excitement and habit to move into action. Again the voice was reminding me: *"All codes and portals are within your bodies. They open at the speed you yourself dare to and are able to receive. This is your journey."*

The next morning I woke up from a dream that was extremely terrifying. I was just about to go back to sleep, not wishing to face this dream, when I, from my inner ear, heard a strong boom, like thunder. I jumped in my bed and was fully awake.

The dream was about my greatest fear –losing a child. In my dream it had already happened. The child was dead. There was fear and despair. My brain wildly started to make all kinds of interpretations. Is there a danger now? Is this an omen for the future? What am I supposed to understand from this?

The voice came, *"You have made yourself sick worrying. How does that go together with your wish to surrender to your Lord God?"*

I prayed to the highest within me. I truly prayed for the child out of love. I did not ask for my fear to be taken away. The rest is to surrender to life and death. I received love from above right into my heart. Slowly, I was getting warm in my body again after being ice cold, when I woke up. Outside, the sea was calm. I went to the cliffs. There was a full moon shining and it was a beautiful start of the day. Frozen and shivering, I cried when I experienced how small I am in this huge universe. I was still experiencing the miracle of receiving this kind of love that holds all of this together. And I think of all mothers around the globe who have lost a child. I cannot imagine a deeper sadness. I felt humility and respect to them for what they go through. There is a lot that I do not understand to the full extent. I felt sick and was not able to go back to sleep. What did this dream mean? Maybe more dimensions? The voice came back: *"Love is what keeps everything together. Without love everything is falling apart."*

My guide came: *"Realise that you are still stuck in certain family patterns!"* I did not want to hear that and thought that the focus had changed in a strange way. After a while I heard the voice of Master K: *"You still keep a part which is judging and condemning others. It is tricky, because at the same time they get away with it, when you take too much on yourself."*

How is all this coming together? I received a flash back and compared to how it was at that point. I saw the patterns clearly, both my own pattern and how that was interwoven with the pattern of others. A strong beam of energy was coming through my head, I received and fell asleep. When I woke up again the daylight was coming in and I realised that the answers will have to wait. My thoughts only mess it all up.

My conclusion is that whatever happens on my part, my only option is to receive from this divine source. It is my purpose to open myself to this source. In the hands of God, I surrender all my tiny attempts to control life. A life that none of us is able to control anyway.

That summer we experienced Mediterranean heat in Sweden and living just right on the beach is like being in paradise. I woke up at ten and realised that I had been taught during a long time in my sleep. I understood that my deeper surrender the other night was needed for this to happen. Devotion, love and faith had made it possible. This is a close co-creation between heaven and earth. The voice is saying: *"This was chosen by you a long time ago due to your love to this earth. Now prepare yourself well! There will be an explosive development on all planes and dimensions. This is just a beginning."*

I recall later that summer beeing in the big assembly hall within the anthroposophist community in a little village south of Stockholm. I am listening to a speech. It is about how we create the future and the possibilities we have to make links with souls on the other side. Being used to being a bridge builder and often inspiring sceptical people, I relaxed and felt at home. Together with so many people and with the message sent out in this natural way was like healing to me. I am not alone and I am not lonely anymore!

I realised then how I have made myself a bit lonely during my whole life regarding my spiritual path. How does that fit with all good friends I do share with on different levels? What I mean is more that I have been cautious, not to be part of an already fixed belief system. I needed to discover for myself to be able to have faith in the reality of many dimensions. And my prayers have come true, to say the least!

I experience and respect how this alternative society has built a kind of prototype that I think will be possible for all of us in a coming future. Of course, it is all up to each and every one of us. The pioneers, Rudolf Steiner and Goethe, were far ahead of their time or you could say they were as wise as some great teachers in the past.

During my days here, I met many friendly people, who wanted to bridge with those of us who have chosen a path outside this special community. And I understood why I was urgently drawn to join the conference.

This was the last day of summer in the cottage and it was time to go home! I am still in bed enjoying breakfast though. The sea outside is grey and calm. The rain is over for this time. The last days have been special as the three first days of the month often are. It started with signals and symptoms, that were not possible to heal with meditation that later turned into a full urine infection. I was in pain, had fever and was shivering. Did I need to see a doctor?

I chose to pull blankets around me and got really warm in bed. I drank a lot of lemon water. As during Christmas, when the stomach flu was in our house, I understood that for me, there was something going on as well in another dimension. I needed to be cleansed and let old fears out, especially on my right side. I asked for help and received. I took very few pain killer, just enough to get the fever down so that I could relax from the pain and be even more available for the light to come in. There was a strong heat and I felt how I was cleansed. In the morning I was tired but without pain. That night I received a visit in a very calm and beautiful way. The light filled all my chakras from above to below and from below to above. I have never in my life felt so whole in my body and as a person.

*"It is completed"*, the voice said. *"You have now received the preparations needed for what will come."*

In wonder, I was thanking and stayed in bed for a long time just receiving the light into every cell. I understood more of what the concept of light body is about.

To turn the summer into city and work life was demanding. I had a lot to integrate and I was very tired. Step by step I got myself together. It was now time for the start up meeting with the leading team at the consultancy company. We started by sharing on a spiritual level before going into actual business matters. That was a good way. We all got nourishment, individually and as a group. Already in the morning, I was receiving from a strong white beam of light. It woke me up reminding me that I had overslept and was late. There was a lot of life and greeting in it. It continued in my shower merging with the sun coming in through the window. My inner forces and energies came back again, as I kept receiving.

When in the city walking from the car to the office, my legs again became heavy. In the stairs right outside the door leading to the office, I suddenly was shown this big room of light beings again, me being one of them there. My spiritual home, the school of Kuthumi! I was blessed. The energy was strong and warm and filled me totally. I needed to stay outside the door of the office to let the experience be fully integrated. I let my eyes rest on the beautiful pattern of the staircase windows, which to me became a symbol of my experience. What a week this was! So intense and so rich! My book was due to be published, I was starting up our company, meetings with different people. I get the support both spiritually and in practice. Millions of details - and I get help.

In the evening there was like a gap in time. There was harmony and it was like time was widened, expanded. I shared this moment with my husband and my youngest son. We sat there together in the sunset in our garden after dinner just talking together. My worlds came together at that point. I am guided and I am guided in a very careful and loving way.

September and October were months of expansion. My book was received in a loving way and got more publicity than I had ever expected. Being a bridge builder by nature, I was especially excited, when I was interviewed a few minutes on a channel that is purely for business people. Using daily common words, I was able to send my message right into the castle of finance in Sweden. The cover of my book can be interpreted in many ways. It is an open hand belonging to someone in a strict suit. In his hand is a glowing golden something. To me he is holding the essence of creation. To others it might be a golden egg or a gold coin. It is all in the eyes of the beholder. The newspapers wrote explorative articles which were of great help to bring the message out at a more profound level.

It was totally clear to me that the book was a product of co-creation between worlds, between dimensions. I have been using my arms, legs, my experiences and talents. Still, this special spark and flow came from another source, surrounding all of it.

This particular time was also a preparation for me to go to India with one of my children, who came to me when she was three years old. We had prepared for a long time to go back to her orphanage where she had spent her first years of her life. Her teenage children were also with us. This journey was a very rich experience for our family and completed a special relationship to adoption and roots.

The other part of that journey had to do with certain threads of my inner life. Already as a little child I was drawn to India without knowing why, except that I met a woman in sari, visiting the little group of pre-school children, that I was part of as a child. My heart was pounding extra then and I had a wish to explore more and find out what this connection was about.

There was another kind of preparation going on that autumn. Independently some of us were during this period of time, given a similar image of Planet Earth pictured as a big lotus. There were many petals around a huge space. People who wished to help each other bring love and harmony to Earth met in this space, each coming from their independent petal.

It was similar also to an image that I have had through many years, seeing all the lights on Planet Earth needing to get in contact with each other in order to raise the frequencies. In those years, when this special inner journey was new to me, I received the following inner vision, giving me direction and meaning for my life:

I saw a sea full of islands like the archipelago outside Stockholm. There were dark clouds over the sky. I saw some lighthouses here and there, some of them were on their own and some of them were closer to each other. Lighthouses are supposed to be of help to travellers on the sea, travelling in darkness and in stormy weathers. I saw a white bright beam of light coming from heaven breaking through all the dark clouds. That light was for everyone on the sea. In my inner vision, the lighthouses were more open to receive the light to bring it further to the sea travellers.

A year after I saw this vision, a friend of mine brought me to the Katarina Church in Stockholm, just because she likes this church. To my big surprise, to the left in the church at a special altar, I found a textile picture showing the same vision.

One early autumn morning I gave myself some extra time for meditation. All my body received light. My stomach received also directly from the light into my navel. I became quite sensitive receiving this nourishment. A voice came: *"This autumn you are completing your responsibilities of being a physical mother. You will still care for them and your grandchildren, but not so much in a traditional way. A chapter in your life is completed."*

*"You are now ´pregnant´ with something that will bloom and be visible six months from now. You will spread the message in different ways before that, but this is special and related to your inner covenant."* And I was filled with loving warmth and heat. I understand that I am experiencing something totally beyond my intellect.

Some days later I woke up from an electric chock hitting my whole body. A voice was saying, *"Now it is time. You asked for it and you get it."* I understood that I am getting prepared for things to come.

*"Yes, we have now planted within you the whole portfolio. It has been going on all night. You don´t understand all of it now. You will know step by step."*

*"It is about sending out light and faith into a world, where human beings are afraid. You will make speeches from November and onwards. Tell about what is needed in the finance crisis. Tell about the difference between hidden fear and trust. Show pictures of the finance crash in the newspapers. Focus on the facts that governments now have to co-operate to solve this. Tell about how human beings are functioning, that these enormous awakenings are needed in order to gather and co-operate. You need to understand that you belong to the same home, your planet!"*

What can each of us do in practice? From the bottom of my heart I realise, that from now on this is my very life purpose to focus on.

I return with my thoughts to my body here in the lovely terrace in Mallorca. It is a warm evening and the moon is full, I saw it rising over the mountains. At the same time I felt a warm wave in my back right between and a bit below my shoulders. This has always been my tender spot. I felt the same warmth, like a warm hand in my back, when I earlier this evening was walking to the little lighthouse in the harbour to enjoy the sunset there. It was like the hand was saying: *"Keep on like this. Just keep forward. All is well!"* This feeling is coming back right now, my light hands lightly touching my heart, giving me a greeting from the androgyne.

The next day I was occupied doing practical things. Just as I was going to write the energies were knocking. This was the third time I was saying: "In a while!" Now, it was time to meet them. And they had important things to tell me. "I´m getting my legs back!" I said out loud, although I was sitting alone at my terrace in my comfortable sun chair. I was sitting with my feet on the chair and my arms around my knees. I was crying out from liberation and joy. I understand now, that I, on one level, have been missing my legs during all my present life. This sounds strange as I, in many ways, am a strong and powerful woman. It has to do with this deep fear, which has been hidden within me. It has shown as a fear of heights, as too much worrying, as a need for planning and control. I have not dared to surrender. What has been hiding my fears is my true loving heart, my idealism, my power to organise and my creativity. I am all of it, including the part filled with deep fear.

Now later, when sitting here at my dinner table with the view over the harbour, my body is soft all over. My legs are carrying me in a new way; I can really feel them from the chair and down to the floor.

*"Your legs are supposed to carry you, so that you can use your arms for flying instead of carrying heavy burdens."*

Those were the words that came to me last summer. The voice also said then: *"Now it is time for your arms and legs."* And I was then shown certain movements and positions via my "light hands", all the time while keeping focus in my forehead and crown, like now.

My experience in my comfortable sun chair today, started with my inner voice saying: *"Now, we are going to take care of your back and your legs."*

And I remember how I this morning woke up while bathing in a hot, calm energy, working exclusively on the right side of my body. Then my light hands made connections diagonally between right and left side of my body. It was a wonderful way to wake up.

When I said out loud, "I´m getting my legs back," and cried tears of liberation, I again experienced a memory from another life time. I was then a soldier in the First World War. In this experience I was coming home from being in the frontline between Germany and Russia.

This memory deep in the cells of my body was first awoken already in the early eighties. I was then in a life situation where I had lost track in so many ways. I had not listened enough to my own needs and I had let myself be caught by guilt. I was about to repeat a pattern that I once had taken actions to break and I was now almost back where I started.

Life is very skilful in the way it teaches you. So was the case also this time. That situation was like a life drama, a scene of life that was repeated for me to awake.

During many years, when I was young, I used to have this certain dream, that I was myself on a train heading somewhere while my luggage was on another train going in another direction. Dreams coming back in this persistent way are very powerful. When I finally took my first tough steps in choosing my own life, giving myself permission to do so even if that was hurting others, then that dream stopped coming. To me at that time, the decision to break my pattern was a matter of life and death.

As I once more was caught in my old pattern the inner guidance came back. So here I was some years later, on my way – of course going by train. As I was standing there looking out of the window, I suddenly discovered a big nerve knot on my right hand. "What is this?" I thought. Today, writing this, I still see the scar from that knot. Often during those years my spiritual brother and I worked as supervisors at a hospital up north in Sweden. As we were both trained therapists, we now and then worked on each other as well. This time I was the client, starting with this nerve knot as my evident symptom.

In the session, my whole body suddenly started to shiver and shake. Then I was moved into another place. I was used to working with guided visualisations, but this was different. I was moved to that place and I became a soldier in a German town. I clearly saw the buildings with all their details. I had just arrived to this town after being in the front line for a long time. I was injured, my legs below my knees were cut, my arms just above my elbows were also cut and I had a wound and a bandage on my head. I was jumping on the street using crutches. In one way I was glad to be back home. Still I had experienced so much of death, killing and dying. I was coming directly from the mass graves. As life is in wars, I had been both a victim and a persecutor.

In front of me there was a man walking. He was dressed in a trench coat from that time. His hair was greasy and disgusting, hanging a bit down the collar of his coat. I became terrified of that man; an ice cold fear rose in me. My whole body was shaking. So was my present body in the session lying there on the bench. I did not see the face of the man in front of me and I would never have dared to either. From that session, I remember that we reached a point where I could sense some thin threads of my lower legs.

I myself, a psychotherapist, tried in many ways to get help to solve this old fear. During twelve long years, as my present life changed into a life I wished to live, I still did not solve this riddle of that old fear. After some years of therapy, I experienced the profile of that man in the trench coat and that profile was the head of a bird, a falcon. That eye of the falcon was only making my terror worse.

Although I was living a good life, this old fear was disturbing me. I felt how this fear was behind my survival strategies in my daily life. In my pattern was a diffuse experience of guilt as if almost everything was my fault. My upbringing had some part in this but not to this extent. On this level it was like I had no right to live if someone else was hurt. I had no right to be happy if someone else was not. I had no right to be in full bloom in case that would make someone else feel not OK.

Sometimes I have needed strong and persistent knockings to wake up from my busy life. I had been shown the work of Ambres already in 1980, the same year as when I had this first experience of the soldier within me. At that time I was not prepared to listen to this offer given to me. Maybe I then found it too special, that an old spirit from ancient Egypt, Ambres, came out in the body of Sture Johansson, an ordinary Swedish carpenter. Still, the teaching that was brought from this was of high quality.

Over a couple of years a client of mine kept informing me about Ambres. When I just listened and did not do anything about it, she finally brought me four video cassettes for me to look at. Then at last I got the message and went to Ambres for a week.

Ambres was working with us as a group during the first part of the day. In the afternoon, we worked on our own, given certain instructions. One such instruction was to paint an animal, a tree and an "egg animal" (a bird). I painted a big tree that partly interfered with a beautiful lake, a scared rabbit and, divided by a line, the profile of the falcon from my experience of being a soldier. The next morning Ambres himself chose what paintings to work with and when. I was the second to go.

During the next ten minutes this whole soldier experience was turned around. Ambres started by giving me a review of my whole life in a few minutes. Then he invited me to sit beside him. He asked me to be the soldier again. I was there within seconds, shivering from terror. Ambres told me to walk to the man in front of me and to pass him. In my experience this was absolutely impossible, but with his guidance I was able to. Finally, I was supposed to look up into the face of the man. I thought I would die. Then suddenly, I started laughing out of relief. I saw my husband Mikael smiling at me. *"Now your shadow has become your guardian spirit!"* Ambres said. I was so relieved that I gave him a kiss on his cheek. *"Don´t do that, I might wish to incarnate again!"* he said with a smile.

After my session with Ambres, many parts of my life came together. It was like a life puzzle coming together where some pieces that fitted the patterns in this lifetime were linked to many pieces from other life times. I became freer in many ways.

Today, many years later, I was not expecting this old lifetime to still be so strongly within me. In many ways I have been living with the experience and thought that I had gotten the help I needed. And so it was, then. However, what has happened during the latest years to me, the woman I am in this life time, has changed the situation. I have had the privilege to receive so much of unconditional love, that I am able to meet the soldier within me in a new way. So this old memory is coming up again, in order to be healed completely.

According to my beliefs we somehow choose our lives, so that we get the learning we need for our soul to mature. In my way of thinking, we come here many times, so that we as individual souls, later maybe as mankind as such, learn. That is why no one is "better" than another. We are all just travellers on our spiritual journeys, needing this earthly "school room" of duality like life and death, good and evil, in order to grow and expand in our consciousness.

My present life started when my parents conceived me just as the Second World War was ending in May 1945. They wished to celebrate by having another child now there was peace. During my whole life I have felt that I came to this world to bring peace. No one has asked me to do this or demanded anything special. I just "knew". I came to a very loving home with parents who wished me well and did the best they could.

What could be a better choice after being in the terror of war? Today, I see how the puzzle fits together. My first childhood memory of the divine presence, when I was four years old, was a way to let me link up again to the divine world that had been cut off from the soldier through the terror he had experienced.

When I was on my way to write about the memory of the soldier, awakened again by the release of old, old tensions in my body, I had to stop, put my pen down and have the little girl from my childhood memory and the soldier meet in a dialogue. This meeting turned into a loving one. Being so much loved in this life, I was able to invite the soldier to a certain place that I had been introduced to in my inner life. It was around the same time as I had this experience with the soldier. However, then I did not understand the gift given to me. Now, being this little girl, I was able to bring the soldier to this special inner place. It is a place, where I see Jesus Christ offer a dome of intense white light. He is just there beside, showing with his right arm, that you are welcomed in. It took me some years before I dared go into that light. I finally did. Now, the soldier within me was welcomed, and he dared to go into the white light.

The soldier and the little girl had a talk together about the terror of war. The little girl was thanking the soldier for having had these necessary terrible experiences and promised: *"You will not have done this in vain!"* Then being the little girl I told him that due to his hard life time, the purpose of my present incarnation is to bring peace and love to Earth. Then the soldier calmed down. I made myself an inner image of how he might have looked like before he was injured and before he was a soldier. He was a young handsome man, who knew little about what human beings are capable of doing from our most destructive parts. In my present life I have always been scared of destructiveness within me and others. Today, I realise how much this is linked to this hard life time of the soldier.

Now this soldier, both being the victim and the evil persecutor, was a part of myself in a loving way. I had taken a further step in healing these wounds. This is what Ambres meant by "shadow" - to welcome and own also parts that are terrible and destructive like this. Otherwise, I project them on others while they stay within me as this kind of old fear. I believe that we as human beings have all parts within us. Living our lives, we are exposed to certain experiences, so that we will be able to integrate these polarities. The last years of my life, I have come more at ease with this. It is easier for me to live and let live, than it used to be. We are mirrors to each other and we learn from that.

Some years ago, after my session with Ambres, a book came into my hands. It was by Elisabeth Haig and the title was "Initiations". It is about her life in Egypt. I felt drawn to that and read the book several times. To my great surprise, I found a picture of what was named the *Horus Falcon.* It looked exactly like the bird head of that man. My heart was beating. There was a clear link. The soldier within me had been looking at the all-seeing eye of Horus and felt unworthy, terrified.

Later I read about this old myth of Isis, Osiris and Horus, Horus being the Christ consciousness within us. There is within me an inner belonging to this old myth and mystery. The Mystery School of Isis in ancient Egypt gives me a feeling of being home spiritually, without my actually knowing that much.

I am now back at my terrace again and the energies are very determined today. I was just on my way to go swimming, when I received a powerful wave coming from above. After a while I understood that it had to do with my need to integrate this whole experience today also on a bodily level. I got that powerful wave, was almost hit by it, when I was sitting in my sofa to put on my sandals. It was a blow to my head and chest that made me fall backwards. That hit was the start of a wave bringing together the energies of my neck and my pelvis. When I laid down to let the energies do their job, it was to me like the highest within me and the part of my body that had been carrying this fear for so long, were brought together. This integration was a very healing experience. My neck and cheeks are now warm. This warmth is flowing to my lower back and is turning into heat.

Something decisive has happened today. Finally this old pattern of mine is released. Again the main force is love. The dark places within us are just places that so far have not been exposed to the light or they have not dared to receive the light. Evil is in fact when we are cut off from the light totally, as was the soldier within me. Still there is a longing for the light. It took me many years to dare to go into the dome that Jesus Christ in my inner image was offering to all of us.

How come that we hesitate? How come that we are just not only running to the light and embrace it? I think we all deep within us know that light and unconditional love is a very penetrating force. It brings all kinds of darkness to the surface. Just as the soldier within me was terrified by the all seeing eye of Horus bringing Christ energy, we all of us avoid to receive love also in daily life. Today, I feel tenderness to this soldier, who had let him get cut off from this kind of love. As the soldier, I felt unworthy after what I had done and experienced and I had lost faith in divine love due to this.

How is this now applied to my daily life on Earth? Even if we all are more or less afraid of the light - some people are more afraid. Some people you even need to shelter yourself from, so that you will not get hurt. Some of them we need to put in jail. Some of them look maybe handsome on the surface but are cold as ice within, totally cut off from feelings, living a life from calculations and using people as objects. In my belief, we all are eventually on our journey to bring in more light in our lives and we all have this divine spark deep inside. The cover is just thinner or thicker. Where there is money or power, more people with thick cover tend to gather. It takes guts to show your open heart there.

In the early stage of my journey, some friends and I agreed on a vision: *"Living Systems – Beholding Life Force"*. Those words are now coming back to me again. First I need to behold my own life force, so that I am able to shelter others, especially children, so that I then will be able to work for life-promoting environments. To do this I need to learn to take responsibility for my negative responses and judgement. This is a hard one. I am learning step by step.

*"Make visible – no revenge"* was something I learnt through some tough experiences way back in my life. I got that sentence in meditation. Those words were of great help later on when I was facing other obstacles.

Today, I shelter myself and others, and I have more courage to just say what I see. For sure, I avoid some environments. However, I do not get as upset as I used to. I even feel tenderness although mostly at a distance. Many may, like me, have a kind of soldier within them, without being aware of it. Many of them are longing for the light much like the mosquitoes in a summer evening are drawn to the light on the table. I see the image how they circle around the light, making noises and getting more and more aggressive.

If you do not dare receive, you will be forever hungry. Out of that hunger we as human beings might do the most destructive and twisted things. Today, I take care of my own need of light and love, getting filled. I try to shelter innocent life wherever I am. I offer a hand, now and then to those who seem to wish that. I try not to interfere knowing that we all have our paths to walk.

I thank the soldier within me for giving me this life enhancing teaching.

10.

# Standing on my own spiritual legs

Here I am again, enjoying my tea and breakfast with a book as my company. This time I am reading "The Human Aura", a book that is said to be channelled from the Masters Kuthumi and Djawl Kuhl. Since the day when I first met Master Kuthumi in my inner world, I have read this book at least ten times, each time understanding a bit more, of course linked to my own inner growth.

This time I am enjoying fresh raspberries with cream along with my re-reading of the book. Suddenly, the bowl with raspberries is falling out of my hands and down to the stone floor. I take care of the broken pieces and what is left from the berries. I tremble. What is this?

Then comes the voice: *"This is no entertainment!! This is important information that needs to get out to people!"*

A bit embarrassed, I think of all the times I have been reading esoteric literature as a way of rocking myself, staying in touch with this world beyond the physical world, as a way to feel at home.

I realise now that a new era is approaching. I need to take responsibility for bringing out into the world, what has been given to me. This is a precious gift. The inner voice is right again. Now I see the pattern even more clearly. There is a pattern described in this book, a pattern of wisdom, that I now have had the gift to experience from inside out.

Tracing back in my diaries I realise that I now had come to a turning point. Parallel to that I am right now stuck in my writing. How come? When I read my diaries from summer and autumn last year I see myself as a woman full of wonder. The treasures unfolding from within are quite provoking compared to what my intellect would call a normal daily life, still my heart, senses and all my cells know the treasures to be true.

I read about my struggle and about my joy. I also read about receiving unconditional love into all my cells. Unconditional love between us as human beings is impossible as long as we live in dualism and as long as we choose not to face our inner fears. There are moments of course when we experience unconditional love between human beings. However those are short moments and then we return to our survival patterns. The endless love coming from inside made me surrender as I have not been able to do before. I understood what bliss is about.

Last year I was guided back to my spiritual home. I recognised many lifetimes. It was like a puzzle, when the pieces come together step by step. As this happened, the intensity of the process raised to a level that was demanding, when it was time to integrate it with my daily life. Still I knew that integration was the whole point of this inner journey.

I am now getting stuck in my writing, because I need to keep certain treasures to myself. For a while, I was into "either-or" thinking, being completely open with everything or to stop writing. However, now I realise that this is not necessary at all. The process itself, when the journey of your soul is unfolding, is an adventure and brings wisdom to all of us and I am more than happy to share that with you.

I return to the point when I visited the orphanage in Bareilly, where my adopted daughter spent the major part of her first three years of her life. As this journey unfolded, I realised that this part of the world had a special meaning for me long before my daughter came to me and our lives were connected to each other. In many ways, life is like a labyrinth. I have met many people, who felt drawn to certain places on Earth. Later they discover deep cell memories from previous lives, provided that they are open to this perspective.

For me it has been like this with Egypt and India, without really knowing why. As a kind of a life riddle, I have been shown details step by step. To me there are no coincidences. There is always a meaning behind events. Writing this I am still on my way to understand the whole pattern. One day, I may be able to know and tell the whole story. Right now I am discovering threads of understanding.

Finally, we have been to the orphanage of my adopted daughter; we were all in wonder of how strong life force is. Against all odds, we were all there together. I have come to believe in guardian angels and this was meant to be. There are forces so much stronger and wider than our human brains are able to perceive. I am very thankful! This was an extremely important moment for my daughter of course, for her children and for me as her mother.

Our tour from New Delhi - Agra - Bareilly and back to Delhi was also like being guarded. Without support, I would certainly be helpless in this special environment. We met friendly people, still it was extremely crowded and cows kept crossing the road on and off. My daughter had arranged a driver with car for this tour. He became like a father figure for us all, cautious and friendly. He was a gift to us in this special, important life situation.

Before going to Bareilly, we visited the Taj Mahal and Red Fort. Being there, something happened to me on a soul level. A special kind of love came to me there. It was with me throughout our days in Bareilly. So wonderful and helpful!

In that evening we celebrated Diwali - an Indian celebration day - much like our Christmas in the West. All restaurants were closed, so we shared our dinner in the hotel room together with our driver. We taught each other words in Hindi and Swedish. We made jokes and laughed together. What a lovely ending of a very special day.

Being in India is like fuel to both my outer and inner life. Within me a strong and sharp energy keeps going through my crown. It is there whatever I do, day and night. I realise that this is part of my path, to learn how to live with this and still keep doing what I do in my daily life. For me spirituality has never been about living a kind of monastery life. Only a break now and then, long enough to be able to listen carefully.

I experienced this while being in Goa. The long beaches make it a very beautiful place and one I really enjoy. Still a couple of days are enough for me. My life is meant to be lived elsewhere. I understand my purpose in life through the beam of energy coming from my inner guidance.

In my heart I know that I have received information of a kind that I still would not understand with my normal intellect. It will stay there and give me impulses later on, impulses that will assist me in the creation of concrete projects.

The following night in Goa was lovely. I spent it in my hammock at the balcony of my room. This warm night under the stars has been a blessing to me. I wake up warm and alert in my body. Something has really happened. I enjoyed walking on the shore and swimming in the waves.

Now I am back in my hammock. There was a strong knocking from this light beam, so I needed to just receive. The voice coming is from Master K. I was taught how to receive energy from this beam of his without "interfering". His way of teaching was linked to a mild humour.

Finally, I was able to let go. *"Keep your focus only on your crown"*, I was told. *"The rest is happening by itself. Never take away your focus from your crown. What is happening in the rest of your body is not your task."* I thanked and surrendered. Again there were vibrations in all chakras and my heart was fully opened.

The next day in Delhi my grandson and I woke up in the morning to the news that Barrack Obama had been selected the next president of the United States. Here we are facing a totally new world. So much heart, inner discipline, vision and honesty! A whole world is filled with hope after years of greediness, misuse of power and corruption. The pictures on TV are speaking for themselves. People are moved, happy and filled with hope, but still down to earth.

"I promise I will always be honest with you about the problems we face." Obama carefully says that we have a long way to go *and* he points out a direction how to. *Together* is the key word. *Now* is time to create what will be the world within the next hundred years. To all doubting and cynical people he says: "Yes, we can." This is truly a day of celebration together with my family.

Later, when I go into myself, I again see the inner vision of this oval with all the petals symbolising development within different areas. We are many people on this Earth, working for the same kind of vision. The time has come when we are to be united. All these beams of light all over Planet Earth that I have been seeing from inside! Now I was also shown that they on the other side are working for the same cause and together with many others. The way of working is the same, only from the other side.

January the coming year will be the start of a new era. The selection of Obama as president of USA is a strong sign. "A new dawn is at hand," he declares. In my personal life, I will enter a new seven year cycle including a more global vision of building and travelling.

It is now a year later. In the evening I am back in my "little nest" after a marvellous day in Palma. It has been a day of completion for this time in Mallorca. I have been to the park, visiting Ionica and the two swans. Close by, some people from Argentina were selling lovely jewellery. I bought a necklace made from beautiful pearls as a reminder of the opening of my throat chakra. I enjoyed the soft music coming from the man playing the saxophone. I also met my friends and colleagues in Palma and I received my final body session for this time. There was wisdom coming together, a link between what my colleague Juan Carlos told me and what I read in my book the same morning. I was shown the link between my pelvis and my jaw and throat. I have a long story of "do it myself", which also means stiff jaw. Now I was again softened all over and now to an extent as never before. I was finally free to tell my truth, now that this old pattern built on fear was released.

I experience the total paradox of life. When I let go of my fear that has stored in my jaw and my pelvis, I am able to be a total receiver. By being a total receiver I am able to speak freely. My throat is opened. Juan Carlos told me that his teacher used to call the heart chakra "the flower" and the throat chakra "the star". These two symbols have been special along my path. He also said: "I have now touched and brought together all your chakras." Before falling asleep I reminded myself to next day go back to the book "The Human Aura". There was something there that I need to look at! - But first my "new" body needs to rest and go to sleep.

The morning after is peaceful. The night has been very long. I experienced a lot of sensations in my body, a process of integration after my body session in Palma yesterday. There was a sense of meaning on many levels. It was like endless polarities were brought together, polarities of the uttermost fear and littleness here on Earth on one side and on the other being carried and lifted by divine love, transformed through the androgyne. Coming home, feeling whole...

Again the symbols of the "flower" (to me a peony) and the "star" come back to me. I read Chapter 11 in the book "The Human Aura". Now I recognise all of it, my whole process leading up to the important point this summer. I understand that the soul within each of us has its own development. This is in the same way as when we grow as physical children. In my spiritual growth I am now finding my own legs to stand on. This means both great joy and great responsibility. This poem beautifully describes the process of the journey of the soul:

*MEDITATION ON SELF*

*I AM no blight of fantasy -*
*clear – seeing vision*
*of Holy Spirit.*
*Being!*
*Exalt my will,*
*desireless desire*
*Fanning*
*flame – inspired fire,*
*glow!*
*I will be the wonder*
*of thyself,*
*To know*
*as only budding rose*
*presumes to be.*
*I see new hope*
*in bright tomorrow*
*here today -*
*No sorrow lingers,*
*I AM free!*
*O glorious destiny,*
*thy star appears,*
*The soul lasts out all fears*
*And years to drink*
*The nectar of new hope:*
*All firmness wakes*
*within the soul –*
*I AM becoming*
*one with thee.*
*(By Kuthumi)*

How I enjoy swimming and experiencing my "new" body! I walk slowly to the beach and feel every inch of my spine and the heat spreading out in my whole body. I feel calm, light and free. Deep within me there is wonder and stillness. On the beach I again met the couple at about my age. They have before expressed to me how much they enjoy their stay in Mallorca.

They had been saving money for a long time and they were now happily adoring every moment. This time when I met them, they were upset about what had happened during the financial crisis, also in Mallorca. We agreed that sleeping well at night, knowing that you at least not deliberately had been trying to cheat, is a great luxury.

This couple reminded me of my parents and their great ability to enjoy wonderful moments in the midst of quite a demanding daily life. This ability is to me a great gift from them and one of many ways to express love. There is truly a wonder in every moment. Often we just pass by and forget to see, hear and feel, what is given to us. Again the ability to receive is the key to life. It is all there, when the blockages of fear do not take away the sight.

I return in my thoughts to the last day in India. We were to leave in the morning. It was a calm morning and I was on my own writing when a mild, loving energy was coming into me through my crown. At that time I recognised the special quality of it, a light, mild and still strong beam of energy finding its way into every cell, reminding me of my inner guides. The journey to India has certainly been about "life puzzles". My daughter has got a deeper understanding of her early history in life. She lost both her parents when she was very little. Unfolding her puzzle, it became very clear that they loved her very much, so wonderful to know!

Within me another kind of puzzle has been going on as well. This puzzle is on a spiritual level. All these threads of understanding will in due time become a more complete pattern.

On our way back home I am one of many passengers on the flight. My granddaughter is sleeping beside me and I am reading in the book "The Audacity of Hope" by the newly elected president Obama. I feel happy reading this book. In my long life I have never heard a president speak like Obama does. I heard a voice of love coming from a position of great earthly power. New winds are blooming! How exciting to be one of many who share this new hope for the world. I feel sure that Obama has a special task in what is happening. Many say global love is what we are experiencing right now. To me this means that we will not survive as humanity unless we learn to love. We are each other and we share the same home, our planet.

Most of us do not change unless we have to. And now we have to. So there will be many tough experiences in the future because we have not been listening very well to the small signals. We will need to learn how to cope with periods of crisis. It goes for us as individuals as well as for organisations and societies.

I understand now that my inner journey is about giving me tools necessary in these times of transformation. I am receiving this with the purpose of paying it forward, meaning giving further to others. I am joining a very intense inner training program. I get it for free and my commitment is to give it further.

I read in my diary about my struggle to cope with two worlds at the same time. I need more and more time to get filled by energies and to be guided. When I do not give me this time, I get tired and the energy gets blocked in my body. At those times I get stiff and feel pain.

Finally, I learned to start by receiving energies and to later do my work. My whole mindset is changing by this shift. I am no longer someone living in the physical world, who now and then, or even daily, goes into meditation. Today, my actual home is in my spiritual world. I am there all day and night whatever I am facing in my physical, daily world.

In the outer, physical world, the financial crisis is evident. Fear is approaching in companies around me, also in the consultant company, where I am the chairwoman. I understand that this is like a test to learn from. Our approach needs to be a combination of facing reality and having faith. Otherwise we would feed the fear and we would thereby create more fear.

Inspiration and creativity don't happen when people only focus on survival. That is why it is so important to find ways how to get away from fear and anxiety. There is a big difference between worrying and staying alert. Energy goes where you put your focus!

Some months after the financial crisis was a fact I spent the whole day with a group of people guided by my friend Doris. Again, I was assisted in keeping contact with my guide, my spiritual brother, in quite a concrete way. My heart was opened even more and the flow became warm and strong. I needed this after a tough period of time at my work.

After these days, being on my own, I ask for directions: *"Your own joy and filling you up with energies are decisive and very important. You cannot be a safety net for others. They have their own work to do. Break loose! They may need to take other decisions than you feel secure with. Be aware not to put yourself in a heavy position."*

*"Be sure to have time and passion for your own drive ahead. You liberate yourself and others through your books and speeches and the network of managers you wish to create. Put your energy there!"*

*"Now that you live more from this spiritual world, it is even more painful to experience all these unnecessary fights. Don´t forget those of your own before! Don´t forget that they are there for us to learn from. Let us now meet through our energies. I am with you, whatever happens, in love, light and joy."*

By this I am filled again with total love and light from my guides. Along with these wonderful energies, I am opened up for a further and wider understanding of my inner world.

Later in the coming night I am woken up by a beam of light coming in through my crown. Extremely slowly, second by second, I receive. It seems like my guides wish to show me that by coming to me while I am asleep, they get beyond my control, thoughts and emotions. They reach me more easily.

Strange, how I go back and forth. One day I surrender, experiencing love, release, and joy. Another day new blockages are coming to the surface to be healed. I read through my notes from my journey to India and the time after. I see the whole pattern and relive these intense moments of creation. I ask for help. Asking for help is one key! I am again able to surrender.

Finally heaven and earth meet within me. Writing this I still feel the pouring energies from my crown to the base of my spine and up again. Finally this inner ice-cold energy has been transformed into heat. The key is love and to ask for help so I can understand how I block myself. My solar plexus is now warm and whole as a fruit. I feel great joy and expectation with no idea what to expect.

It has been a great release to go through what happened during summer and autumn last year. I realise how intense this time was, how I was brought into a totally new world within me. It was a world of love, light and joy. I felt younger and happier than ever. Still then, I found no ways how to link these experiences into my daily life. I was totally on my own.

Now I feel free also in my writing. I hope that some of you reading this will benefit from what I share. Hopefully, you will be supported to trust your own inner experiences. We are travellers together in our spiritual journeys. To me this is the most important. Many people that I have met are doing the same as I did. They interrupt their inner journey by not trusting what is happening to them.

I understand that there is a meaning behind why I have been struggling so much by living in two worlds at the same time. It is about bridge building on many levels and within many dimensions. I learn to be like an instrument, a kind of vessel, for this bridge building to happen. My task is to stay connected and not block the passages within my bodies.

Although I sometimes find living in two worlds to be quite exhausting and painful, I need to learn these skills. Being a bridge builder between worlds is my life purpose. And I am very well taken care of with great love while learning.

11.

# Manifestation in the outer world

I have been through a very special night, a kind of completion. The little candle in its box is still burning. I keep it here on the terrace; I feel that I do not want to put it out. Beside the candle is also a peony, this beautiful symbol so essential to me.

Until four this morning I stayed at the terrace. The night was mild and warm. I had been deeply engaged in my writing, an exciting task. Sitting here in the night my light hands were again giving me one of their inner sessions. They showed me how different parts of my physical and energy bodies are linked together. This inner map of energy points is getting more and more understandable to me.

I was shown how my root chakra now is free from fear. Extremely calm and still I was filled with soft energies and warmth. Then the inner voice came: *"Good that you are writing! Important information to be spread! What you cannot write about right now, is the content of your inner mysteries. Still don´t forget that these mysteries are the essence of what is happening. You will understand more later on. When you heal yourself, others are healed at the same time. We are linked to each other. This is our greatest responsibility. So don´t forget the mysteries, just because you are so eager to write."*

How true! I easily go into doing instead of just being with what is. So now, I just sit here and let myself be "bathing" in this lovely energy of connections. I leave my thoughts and realise that whatever the pattern may be, *love* is the answer, the reason and the healing force. Again it was crystal clear to me, that the whole purpose of this inner journey was to fully understand what love is.

I was invited to a ceremony last night by an intense energy beam coming into my crown. All my chakras were brought together and finally I experienced myself like the tiny little fairy tale girl Thumbelina living on a leave, receiving with my whole body, as if I was a bowl. My feet spontaneously met each other, my knees out to the sides like small babies do. A flash of a thought went through my mind. I remembered that I had never been able to sit in a traditional lotus position while meditating. Now my body knew by itself. A voice came: *"Now we are opening your throat chakra fully. Time for you now!"* My light hands by themselves made a bridge between heart and throat in different angles. At the same time I experienced a new kind of quality of energy coming to me through my crown. It was faster, sharper and hotter. I felt blessed.

A new chapter of my inner journey is taking place. I have received what I need, so that I myself am able to contact the spiritual world. Love is creation - that is what it is all about. I have expressed my "yes" from the bottom of my heart and I have received tools.

December last year was tough in many ways. As a reaction of working too hard, I was frozen and stiff in my body and was longing to give myself time to surrender to my inner world. I also felt like I had been living in a kind of incubation period. I had been restless and impatient, signals I well recognise as time to go away.

Finally, a few days ago, I expressed my need inwards. Again and again I receive the same truth: *"Ask and you will get!"*

The day before New Year's Evening, a voice came to me in the morning: *"Keep your focus now in ajna, your forehead. Let Master K do the rest!"* This chakra became more and more vibrant. I was guided to hold my light hands on two certain points on my arms. When they found the right spots, suddenly, a cascade of energy and light went from these spots up to my forehead and crown and back. My whole upper body became soft. Then my light hands moved to the spots of my thighs that had been ice-cold for several days. *"Keep your focus on your forehead!"* I heard again. I was shown, how I consciously could send beams from my forehead to areas in my body needing light. This was a moment to moment process of encounter between the two places. The inner teaching went on for a while and the cold places became warm and soft. Not all of them though. It was like a beginning. Some of the places became hot. I thanked my inner guides for the teaching. I felt that I had been visiting the inner school of Kuthumi that night.

Later that day was like magic. I kept learning the skill of using this big vibrating forehead chakra for healing my body. My head was heavy from energy and I felt a bit dizzy. I learnt how to listen carefully and be a total receiver.

Now in the evening of New Years Day, the energy flow is extremely strong. I notice that ajna, my forehead chakra, has stabilised. I am now living from there most of the day, giving constant healing to the rest of my body. Step by step the last frozen spots have softened.

The spinning of the web between me and my soul friends is ongoing. I emailed my friend Jorunn in Den Haag and suggested a meeting there at the end of February this year. At once a strong flow of energies came to me as a kind of confirmation. Marie, my friend and colleague, met with me yesterday. The theme coming up was that there is a need of a modern kind of mystery school suited to people of today. In the midst of daily professional and family life many people that we meet are longing for more nourishment to their souls. Johannes phoned me yesterday evening. He had been thinking of me a lot during the latest days. Threads are coming together creating the web. New Year's Day is the start of a year that will be turbulent and exciting.

Last night a kind of breakthrough happened. I still feel the waves in my body. I had asked for help again and got the impulse to wrap myself in a blanket, sheltered, and let myself be taken away for the night. I fell asleep. I woke up during the night by a beam of energy coming to me via my neck and crown. Certain spots on my arms and legs were activated. A heat was spreading all over my body. I got the message again that all knowledge is downloaded in my body, not the least in my bones and arms. It functions like a transformation system. Via my light hands, my legs are activated as well as all my chakras. I was also told that now I did not any more need my sexuality in a traditional way. All chakras have come together and my throat is activated.

Finally, I went to sleep again. I had put two alarm clocks besides each other so that one would start ringing before the other. I knew that I like to have some time to wake up. I did wake up to the first one and switched it off. Then I surrendered to the intense loving energies going through all my chakras. Now finally my legs were totally warm and soft. When I came back to this reality I looked at my two alarm clocks. What had really happened?

One way or another, the clock hands had changed on the second clock. It was ringing as I had set it to do, but it showed a different time to the first one. Last evening they were the same. This experience reminded me of when I was in Mallorca a couple of years before and experienced a gap in time.

What is time? In the extended and widened *NOW* the usual experience of clock time disappears. In those moments time and space are gone. We are in eternity. Maybe we are there all the time and just do this construction of time and space, while we are living in the third dimension of dualism? Still we need this dualism for us to learn.

I realise that clock time certainly is not there when I am intensely guided as now. Again I learn that it is up to me to ask for help, to decree. When I do this from a pure heart, I am heard and receive far beyond what I could ever imagine. Then my task is to surrender and receive from this source. All wisdom is already placed within me as it is for all of us. What an ingenious path!!

Some days later I feel new blockages. I am filled with energies; still something is stuck in my thighs again. I am also stuck in my daily life as I keep holding myself back. Today I need to live who I am. My old pattern of control coming back again is expressed as exaggerated considerations both at work and in my family. I need to claim the right to my own life. No one else can do this for me. This is my own job! A voice is coming to me, after my decree and expressed willingness to meet what will come: *"Are you prepared? You must choose more clearly! You must give more time and focus to your inner life. Still you get lost both at your work and at home. There is no space for this anymore! Prepare the way!!! Make space!!!"*

I decide to give myself help and guidance. I book a session with someone who will be able to assist me, so that I will stay true to myself.

Later there was a cleansing of blockages in my relationships both at home and at my job. The answer to my commitment of cleansing came directly. I got help in the most precious way. In my morning meditation, I heard a voice like talking to my forehead: *"Lift yourself - higher!"* The voice came back several times, repeating those words. I was able to raise my energies. The answer came through a mild, loving energy spreading through all my chakras. I saw inside of me a light and in that light I saw a vision of Jesus Christ. *"Remember, I have always been with you in tough times. – Receive and you are sheltered!"* I let go of my control, I cried from joy and old sadness and I surrendered.

The day after looking at TV I take part of the inauguration of President Obama as the new president of USA. This is truly a new era. So much of hope in the world! Not even the most cynical people can stop this joy. At home my husband Mikael and I share this moment, both with tears of joy. I feel like being part of a huge network around our globe. All these people sharing the hope of a better world built on the fact that we need to co create or we will destroy our planet. This is an expression of love, to me a coming back of Christ energy. This special day and moment was like a collective lifting of energies.

Some days later on a Saturday morning I am still in bed. Last night I was not able to fall asleep. I was full of energies. I had cleared out things both at my job and at home. I came home from working with a group of managers for a couple of days. This was a meaningful job and I was not tired. Instead this free energy turned into thoughts and patterns. I got more and more focused and wrote a few lines about what I called "A Mystery School of Our Time": "The mysteries of life cannot be understood unless we investigate with our whole being as an instrument. Our senses, our feelings, our consciousness are the tentacles, when a soul is finding its way home. Each of us has her journey to do. Every journey is unique. Each of us has her understanding within her own context. We wish to offer good tools for this inner journey, powerful and healthy tools to assist each one to find her own spark of life. The mystery school of our time does not teach a certain religion. Important is however to keep an open mind and your own longing for an inner journey. The power of creation is within each of us. It is about discovering how this force can be used for different purposes to serve the wholeness and Earth. There are different entrances and paths for each of us."

What I wrote last night was a kind of manifest of what is to be created and already exists in the ethereal world.

Suddenly the telephone is ringing. Doris is on the line. She had been talking to Jorunn suggesting that we will meet in Den Haag at the end of February. Later we discovered that all three of us had been woken up at half past three during last night. In our different ways we all got the message to go to Den Haag during that time. I recognise the spirit of my inner guide, my spiritual brother in this. My heart is making jumps of joy. NOW it is happening!!!

Yes it did happen! The February meeting was manifested as we were told. How do you describe the moments when your dreams come true? How to tell about when energy that has been building up for a long time is coming together and finds way to become a reality in our physical lives?

Writing this I am sitting in a chair looking over the beach of the North Sea. The few days spent had been like a month. The veils between this physical world and the other side have been extremely thin. A true co-operation in a group form has taken place. We have been carefully and lovingly guided.

We have recorded and later I took notes of what was said about the fundament for further building of our coming project.

February 23 was my birthday. On a personal level I got the most precious gift. I received pieces of my inner life puzzle. In the afternoon we were both resting, when Doris suddenly was knocking at my door. My guide, my spiritual brother, had approached her and given her what he called "rebuses" for me to solve.

Doris was hesitant about what they could mean. *"It will give meaning to Barbro!"* my guide had told her. And it did. I was so relieved. My critical, doubting part had to go to rest. I was deeply thankful! During the latest days my inner covenant, that I had kept to myself for such a long time, was now shared and visible to my two friends. My soul was truly heading home.

In the following afternoon, I went for a walk by myself along the shore of the North Sea. Doris was resting and Jorunn was with her children. I was restless. I knew that something was on its way concerning the name of this becoming organisation. As I walked and gazed over the horizon, I saw a big pier in front of me. Intuitively, I wished to go there to get an even better view. Standing there overlooking the big sea, I heard inside of me the name of this new non-profit organisation. It came easily to me: *"New Era College."*

When you know that something is right, there is a special feeling in your body. So it was for me. I quickly phoned to Doris and Jorunn, who had been part of what had happened during the recent days. They were both happy about the name. Then I called Johannes, Marie and Peter, all colleagues and friends, whom I knew would be natural parts of this. Within a short time I had reached all of them. They all said their yeses in a way as if they had been waiting for this, naturally and with happiness.

Later Justo was to be the seventh founder. Justo is a Bolivian Indian, a medicine man from his tradition and a close friend to Johannes. In her readings, Doris had been seeing both Johannes and Justo without knowing them physically in advance.

On my way back to the hotel from my walk along the shore, I felt extremely happy. I had been totally true to the singing of my soul. Then this special happiness is the answer. A voice came to me: *"Stretch your back besides being thankful! You are part of what is happening. This is a co-creation between worlds."* "True - and it is about mutual love", I thought walking my way back to the hotel.

Being here in Mallorca is a natural result of the guidance I just described. This evening I will meet Johannes, his wife and two other colleagues. It is a pleasure for me to get to know these friends and colleagues. I see many new possibilities of co-operation.

By being here I get to know how my colleagues are building their centre. Johannes has already been working in Sweden for many years. My friend Jorunn is in Holland, Justo in Bolivia, Peter in England. I get the vision of several centres like these in different countries working together, still each having their own clear fundament. I realise that the organisational form will be more of a network than a college. Later we decided to name the organisation the New Era Net. We are starting all this by assisting each other in what we are doing. This nourishment is like nutrition for flowers to grow. Then the plants are growing. Being here in Mallorca experiencing the network growing, I understand more and more why I need to learn Spanish.

12.

# A new calling to another dimension

I am enjoying this last summer day in Mallorca 2009. It is a hot day. I need shelter from the sun. Tomorrow I will be back in Sweden, where there is now a chilly autumn.

The whole morning I have been experiencing calm, healing energies. I was woken up at eight by a beam of light coming into my wrists at the place where you can feel your pulse. Time for a new inner session!

This time I was in a systematic way shown the spots I need to know, so that I by myself am able to raise my energies. It was like a repetition of the inner ceremony from yesterday. This finger positioning, the androgyne, wakes up all the chakras and also other energy spots. I was shown this pattern of energy spots, so that I would remember in times to come, when my daily life demands more of me.

The day after coming home from my stay in Den Haag in late February this year, I saw a special symbol in the sky. I was doing routine things, like buying food for my family. When I came out from the shop, I stopped and put my bags in the snow. In the sky among the stars I saw a quarter of the moon lying down with a big star right above it. This was one of these magic moments. I recognised this symbol. To me there was a meaning behind it. I still don´t know for sure what. A few years back some of my New Era friends did a group meditation to find a symbol for our common vision. We ended up with the same symbol as I saw that winter day in the sky. When we at that time put words to this symbol, we called it "Living Systems - Beholding Life Force".

Now sitting here at my terrace in Mallorca, I have again been reading parts of the book "Hathor" by Tom Kenyon and Virginia

Essene. This book came into my hands two years ago. I was stunned when the first thing I observed was this symbol being the basic theme of the book.

After my morning meditation, I kept my husband Mikael in focus. I so much wished for him to experience the same kind of unconditional love from inside as I do. But who am I to tell. Maybe he is already experiencing it? Still I was wishing this for him. *"Through you!"* was the rapid answer to my wish. Where did this voice come from? I asked to be able to meet Mikael´s higher self from my own higher self. There he was again, as I had experienced several times before, an old Tibetan man looking at me with a twinkle in his eyes.

"Is it true that I will be able to inspire my husband in this?" I asked. *"Yes, now that you yourself have learnt what love is!"* I gave him right in this. My love has been with my husband all these years, but is has been mixed with my deepest inner fears.

We have shared a long life together in the spirit of providing shelter for one another. Like most love couples, we ground each other's inner diamonds in a profound way.

There will be no peace on Earth until our hearts have been cleansed from fears and the strategies we use to control those fears in order to survive. Intimate relationships are our greatest teachers.

Then I hear a voice I recognise well: *"Remember that nothing of this would have been possible unless you yourself had opened your heart and longing. Your wishes beyond your selfish needs and passion have been the start of all this!"*

The voice continues: *"Now you have your <u>flower</u>, your <u>star</u> and your <u>bowl</u>. You are prepared to go out in the world and build "stars", like you have been doing already. Build groups from this energy. The power in a group of seven, becomes seven times itself, seven times. These stars become like meeting points between worlds and contribute* *to the evolution of the planet Earth. Your book will be spread and be of help. It is needed now."*

The fog that surrounded me the whole morning, has now lifted. Many things are clearing up for me in many dimensions. From my husband I heard last night that the new floor in "my" part of our house is in place. This means to me a peaceful place in my home for my inner life. This concrete foundation is needed for me to be able to fulfil my inner task. Now time for a swim!

After the intense days in Den Haag, when what is now the New Era Net was conceived, I have been living like I was in fever. I tremble and I wonder if all this will fall concretely into place. My five years of inner guidance is now reaching its completion phase. I understand that one of the dimensions of completion will be to create this organisation. I realise even more now that these inner mysteries are the kernel of what is happening.

Today I send out formal invitations to the people, my soul friends, who have said yes to the suggestion that we meet and give birth to the coming organisation. I invite them to a meeting in Stockholm in June. The following three nights were extremely intense. Wrapped up in my blanket I experienced being transported to my spiritual home, experiencing rich, necessary and loving contact. My soul´s life pattern is being revealed. Gradually I relax in the inner knowing from the other side. I feel like I am coming home from an extremely long journey that has lasted eons. During one of these nights I was told that my guide was going to contact the others in my group of soul friends about the meeting in June.

One morning some weeks later the voice finishes the inner session by saying: *You will gradually become younger. This is not a woman of age sixty and you will become even younger."* It was true to me. My whole body was electrified. I enjoyed this feeling of being vitalised.

I am in my physical life gaining a lot from being uplifted. I continued this morning by shuffling a lot of snow, so that I could go to work by my car.

Later the same evening the voice comes back again along with an intense "waving" of the candle light in front of me:

*"There are mysteries that have been kept from most people. They are about subtle energies in the encounter between worlds. They are about how sexual energy is transformed into creation when it meets and merges with energies of higher frequencies.*

*This is also how all kinds of true art are created. This is the deeper meaning of the kundalini force. Over time, people have distorted and perverted these energies. Time has come for more people to get in touch with this. Theosophy had this intention. However, it partly turned into something else.*

*We will teach this through ourselves. That is why you need to get used to this. I am with you in your energy body. Relax and don´t think in an earthly way around this completion. There is a plan and all is well. Your friend Justo from Bolivia is a wisdom keeper of these mysteries. You will get support. Remember – your own inner task of life is what is most important."*

Some weeks have passed and it is now early spring. Today is a special day. Now all my friends invited to join me on 12 and 13 June 2009 have confirmed that they are coming. I trembled with joy when I read their emails and talked with them on the phone. They all expressed their deep commitment to this event. Many threads are coming together and they seem to all work out for the best. I am in wonder when I think of how all this works. I am part of something far beyond my intellect. I am gradually learning to surrender to this pattern from other dimensions. I am learning just to respond with my intention coming from my true and loving heart.

Recent weeks have been strange; I feel like I have been living in two worlds. I have been confused and forgotten things. I end up driving in the totally wrong direction etc. What I am living now is not possible to tell others as it might be misunderstood. I need support.

So today I feel happy that I have booked time with an old friend and spiritual guide, Marina, later in April. I need it. I struggle with integrating my inner world with my daily life. In a way I would like to spend some weeks in a monastery on my own. At the same time I know that the challenge to also be in a daily life is part of my learning. In my inner life I get all the love and nourishment I need. It is clearly my job to face my family, my colleagues and clients with the strong experiences that live in my heart.

Before going to meet Marina, I went through an important milestone in my family. I had for some reason scheduled yesterday to stay home. During the day, my husband Mikael took the initiative suggesting we did a meditation together. I was happy to join him. This turned into a very rich experience. Mikael experienced a light being behind him and I saw it with my inner mind. Beside me I felt the presence of my guide, my spiritual brother and behind I experienced the presence of Christ. I asked for help and blessing and my wish that Mikael would receive the love of Christ. We shortly opened our eyes after meditation and looked at each other for a long time. We shared our experiences and found a loving way to be with each other, honouring each other´s life paths.

The same day, the decision was made about an apartment for our youngest son. He was now ready to move to create his own life, leaving home. A liberation for him and a liberation for me, knowing that he is proud and happy.

This new phase in life for our family means that I have more space for my inner life. My responsibility of being a physical mother in daily life is over. My focus now will be on my spiritual journey and what this journey might bring about. In our home this means also physical change. The visible changes go along with inner, invisible changes, especially in phases of completion.

Later one night I experienced an inner meeting with my guide, and with Peter, one of my friends coming to the June meeting. In the morning I again contacted my guide. There is a special inner place where I easily meet him. Spontaneously, I put my left hand beside me. Through the years I have often felt his hand in mine.

This time there was no hand in mine. Curiously, I listened to be guided. *"We will now meet in another way. Raise your energies yourself!"* I brought my hand back and raised both my hands to my heart. Then the energy came to my heart and filled me. The exchange was strong. A powerful beam of light came via my forehead and heart to the rest of my chakras and organs. My whole body was vibrating. *"You are being prepared!"* the voice said. In that moment I was a total receiver. The inner covenant was thus confirmed each day and night. I was living it in every moment.

A few weeks later I am home again after a visit to Marina, my friend and spiritual guide. I feel calm now. This visit to her has been extremely important and necessary. Without my saying anything, she saw what was happening to me and was able to give me valuable support. Finally, I was not making myself lonely in this world concerning the inner mysteries. Such a relief! And I got clear instructions from Marina, instructions that I knew to be true. "You must give even more room and space to go higher in your energies! You are part of something where you depend on each other. You need to be clear and focus on your inner life purpose! Keep on doing your light exercises," Marina told me. "This is how you build your light body." She spoke of these inner exchanges of energies that I had been keeping to myself for years as a kind of secret and treasure.

In the session with Marina, I was strongly in contact with energies linked to Mother Mary. This female guidance was of great help to me. I realised that I have been neglecting the wonderful support that had been there all the time. Now I was so happy to take part of her power and wisdom.

Spring is approaching also in a Northern country like Sweden. It is now the end of a long lovely weekend. The container outside our house is now filled with old things to be thrown away, things from the basement of the house and from our garage. Important steps!

Cleansing has taken place also within me. I sent old destructive forces to the volcanoes in the inner part of Earth. And I called in light and sun energy. I also decided to cleanse my body. I started a diet to make by body happy. I needed a physical body that was in line with my inner world.

My husband Mikael and I again shared a meditation. We were both taken far away. We were able to share with each other in a loving way. I saw him in the Himalayas and the landscape around him.

In my inner life, the passage becomes freer. I heard a voice saying: *"Now I am able to reach you all the way!"* I understood that the passage within me now was free. Together with these words came a powerful beam of light through my crown, my hands, my armpits and went in waves all the way to my root chakra. It truly was like the passage was freer. My skin is also getting more and more sensitive, like hundreds of small spots activating energy, like electricity. While this is happening, I also hear ringing sounds in my ears.

I realise that when I take care of my daily life, being true to who I am today, the intensity from inside becomes stronger. Being like a radio station, I need to be responsible for my ability to receive in a clear and strong way.

It is now in the evening of a Saturday in late May. I woke up early today, already contacted from the other side. Receiving these energies was bewildering to me. Again there was this vibration, the sounds, the electric feeling. I was far beyond this physical world.

The voice came back to me again, and I knew this to be an important moment: "*Creation happens where and when the polarities meet in the trembling very moment. When the energies meet there, and you are able to stay in the void, something new is created. This is what your teaching is about. The polarities are between dimensions, between male and female energies. You have cleansed yourself, so that we now can come to you in this way. Everything is now about preparation. You will understand more later.*"

I was able to stay in the now moment and not for a second go ahead of it. By doing this I was filled with very intense and vibrating energies. I stayed in this transmission for a couple of hours (as I understood later). I was dizzy and my body was transformed. My whole body was over-sensitive and electric, my head was heavy and filled, as was also my throat. I felt like old, old tensions were going away.

The rest of this day, I spent in my sun chair in our garden. I was overwhelmed and had to digest what had happened. I was not able to do anything but just stay in the sun, resting.

Lying there, I saw my life pattern mirrored in my body. The guidance from Mother Mary had cleared my eyes. I was finally ready to let go of the old pattern of how I had been living as a woman in this lifetime. Like all women, I too have the right to be beautiful, radiant and divine. This sounds maybe very natural. However, not until this late in my life have all my bodies lived this truth. I have been travelling a long way to come to this day.

It is now the very last hours of my visit to Mallorca and I have moved to stay the night in the nearby hotel before flying out early tomorrow morning. I am now facing civilisation again after the last weeks in my little nest and my intense living in other worlds. I was almost shocked when I entered my comparatively fancy big room in the hotel. It is a good decision to make my return home in steps!

Johannes phoned me and wished me good journey back home. He told me about small tornados in Puerto de Andratx. I had only noticed this fact in the moment I said good-bye to "my terrace" and was giving thanks for all the intense sessions I had been experiencing there. Then a strong wind came and I had to bring everything inside.

This evening I had dinner at the hotel restaurant in a nice and cosy corner. Sitting there I "happened" to hold my hands tied together as the androgyne above my knees. Then I discovered the healing capacity of my hands being in this position. A strong heat spread all the way down to my feet. It was like life was coming into my legs below my knees. Again I reflect how much has happened during these days. I am standing on my two spiritual legs as well as my physical. I have received tools. My throat is also alive in a new way.

What a contrast to my despair on that July night five years ago when this inner journey started! I realise also that there have been years of preparation in my life before this special journey.

Slowly, I am changing my focus in direction of home. One part of me would like to just stay, continuing to write. The other part of me knows that I need to wait and come back later. The process of my present life is part of my writing. Process, within process, within process...

Yoghurt, thé con leche, naranja natural...At Palma airport I am enjoying a nice and peaceful breakfast after having gone through the security gates. This time there was no problem concerning excess weight. The lady put a label "heavy" on my suitcase, but I did not have to pay extra. The security control reminds me of all the traumas in this physical world. After my precious days in Mallorca I experience this as even more absurd, although I realise the necessity. When I was on my way to put my things in the box on the security line, I saw another "box" just after me in the line. It was a little baby of about three months looking at this strange dance the adults were doing. How much does the baby, so newly arriving from the other side, understand? What a world to get into!

Before leaving, I thought my trip home would be a way to catch some more sleep. Instead the energies are intense throughout the whole trip. I get the feeling that the inner sessions are here to tell me all that I need to know before I will be home facing a much more demanding world.

My hands tied as the androgyne keep giving me healing. The heat is spreading step by step all throughout my body. The teachings that started yesterday in the restaurant is continuing. Meanwhile my thoughts wander on and off as a way to assimilate these precious days.

Later I told myself that now is time for sleep. My day started very early. Spontaneously, I held my left hand around my right elbow and rested my body to my left side. My right hand fell down and landed on the inside of my right knee. Slowly, slowly, this position made me relax in a totally new way. Along with this, my inner process is also going to peace through a deeper understanding.

This is in the evening after the culmination in the Stockholm June meeting 2009. I did not write anything in my diary the two weeks before. This is no coincidence. I remember those weeks as being more than intense. From inside the energy within me was raised to a very high level. I used all the wisdom I had so that I would be able to keep this level inside of me and still do my regular work.

The two days just before the meeting with the New Era friends were used for team-building of the leading team of the consultant company. Peter, who was also coming to the meeting, worked with this group of consultants, giving us new perspectives from his great spiritual sources.

My other friends coming to give birth to the new organisation were arriving, so there were guests at my home. I tuned in with them how to work during the coming days, this special event. I decorated our seminar room with peons and candles.

When I woke up in the morning during those days, I felt dizzy and experienced something like a white fog in the room. My energy and my excitement were raised more and more by the day. Within me I knew this to be the completion of my five year long special inner journey with my spiritual brother as guide. Even in my body I felt as if I were giving birth to something, although of course on an energy level, and linked to the coming project of this group of soul friends.

Writing this at the end of the two days, I reflect on what actually happened. Yesterday, it was manifested. It was truly a day of wonder. Doris, being a medium, gave a reading to each one of us as a gift and a way for us to get to know each other and to come together.

Later, Justo made a ceremony of flowers. He took the vase with the seven peonies, holding it with both hands, letting male-female energies come together. Each of us had a moment of holding the vase, breathing in the beauty of and the essence of the flower. Worlds were coming together.

I was the last one to hold the vase. I felt like two hearts were coming together as one. My heart was burning. The waves went out to the others in the group. Deep within me I got a knowing that love is the essence of creation. The basis of everything. Love is what keeps our universe together.

This ceremony was the actual birth of what is now the New Era Net. Most of us continued the next day as well. We shared meditations of our vision of this newly born organisation.

What one of my friends shared after a meditation woke up a deep cell memory within me. For a while I was gone. I could not move. I heard myself tell the others: "Yesterday, my heart was burning. Now my whole body is burning and this is going out to you as well." During the last thirty-five years of exploring life, I have been through many strong experiences. However, this was like nothing else. I heard my friend Doris saying: "She is being overshadowed."

I could not speak about this. I just had to leave the room for a while to integrate the experience within me. Some of the others were a bit worried. However, I was back within a few minutes, lighter and happier than ever.

Now my inner journey had reached a completion. I was happy, I was happy for my guide, my spiritual brother. Now we were both free to continue our own paths, he on the other side and I in my physical life.

After these two intense and precious days, all seven of us spread to the wind. It was like we all needed lots of time to digest what had happened to each of us and together.

Right now I can hardly grasp what we have been through together. I know that I will need time. I know that I will need to write to be able to understand and integrate what has happened. I have a long summer by the sea ahead of me. I need it. In the meantime I seal all my diaries from the last five years in a bag until I am ready to open it.

Twenty-five minutes before landing at Arlanda Airport my thoughts go to the heavy bag that I took to Mallorca. I have now read all my diaries from five years back and I have finally been able to receive the treasure I got. I have got perspective and guidance so that I will be able to transform the gift into my life purpose.

I become aware of an inner dialogue. It is like my hands are talking to each other. Very still and calm, my left hand is moving over my right hand touching between the sinews. An intense heat is spreading through all my chakras. It is filling my "bowl".

Now I notice that my left hand has been moving to the next space between my sinews. There is the scar from the nerve knot, which I discovered thirty years ago. That nerve knot was the symptom that started my remembrance of the incarnation of me being a soldier in the First World War.

The heat is continuing to spread. Now it is also coming to my lower legs and down to my feet. My legs are now being filled with life. I am healed from the wounds in that life that was full of terror. My fear will no longer hold me back. I am free to be open to life in all dimensions.

Life is a great wonder! As many times before during these five years of my inner journey, I am stunned. And now the heat is flowing intensely from above filling the whole of me. I need to put my pen down…

Am I being overshadowed in the midst of landing at Stockholm airport?

# TRACING WISDOM

- Reflections and learnings from my inner journey -

# PERSPECTIVES

Today I know that I forever changed as a human being on that day in July 2004, when I was invited to join the inner spiritual journey, which I have shared with you here in this book. No wonder all these years had to pass, until I now feel ready to publish and share with the world around me.

Of course my inner journey continued while I was writing this book. Time wise, the first part was not written in twelve days, but over almost one year. So it was like a triple process while writing. However, that would be too complicated both to write and read. The breaks were necessary. In the meantime I gained further inner understanding, so that I was able to write.

The latest break was from summer 2010 until winter 2011. The first part was written. Still I was not ready to publish. I started to write the second part, but the flow was gone. Now I realise that I had to live through some special learning during the year 2010 before the time was right to publish.

It is now early spring 2011 and I am ready to share with you. If we would meet ten years from now, there would probably be even more wisdom to share about what has happened during these years.

**It is all in the eyes of the beholder**

In my view we are all just souls on a life journey. My intuition tells me that we are here on Earth to learn and develop as souls. We need this third dimension of duality to mature as souls. So we come back many times to learn from being here on Earth.

We need all kinds of lives to be able to mature. Some souls are younger than others. Still we are travelling together, often in groups, and often with a special purpose.

What I like about this view is that it takes away every attempt to compare between us. No one is better than anyone else; we are just on different journeys experiencing different things. In my view this is a maturing transformation for mankind. My vision is that all souls, when refined, are heading towards the source we all came from. In essence we are all one!

As my reader, please feel free to believe in whatever is right for you. If you feel provoked, just jump that part and move on! I am not here to preach or sell a kind of religion. I am here to tell my story and what I learnt from it. I trust that the freedom I feel by finally sharing my story will inspire others to do the same.

In my business practice, I have met many people, who have had the same kind of experiences as I now share with you. Many do as I did for many years, they hide being afraid that people will ridicule them or look upon them as crazy. I hope that this book will assist them to dare be open. If we wish an open society, we need to accept that people might have experiences that are not shared with the kind of truth blessed by the present authorities in society.

In the old days, the church told people what to believe in. So it still is in many Muslim and Catholic countries. In societies like the Scandinavian, we have developed a new kind of church, as I see it. Science has taken on the role of telling people what to believe in. However, not even science has all the truths. It depends on context, level of consciousness, values, areas of science etc. Who is able to scientifically explain the essence of love? Still, this is the main force in life for most people, whether you are lucky to receive love and give love, or you have a life lacking the experience of love.

I believe that we all need to be humble, while we trace the wisdom we get along our life path. One way is to just share and listen to each other. Every person is unique and every person brings a life story into the world. We might find that as well as being unique, we also share experiences that we recognise from each other. Then we add a bit to the general wisdom of being a human being.

**Perspective on everyday life**

When I read through the story of my inner journey, I again and again notice the struggle I had when it came to integrating my intense inner world with my daily life, both family wise and work wise. Still, I knew all the way, that it was meant to be like that.

Today, I am at ease with this struggle. In fact, I am thankful beyond words, for what I have received during these years. There is harmony in my family with all these warm, loving people going on with their lives. It is such a gift to be able to enjoy them all at their different ages from two years up to seventy. Together my husband and I now have a family of twenty people, although in daily life there is only the two of us.

My working life changed a lot through the inner journey described in the first part of this book. I learnt how to co-create with life itself instead of, as sometimes before, going against life. Amazing things happened. Life became like an unexpected movie and it was exciting to see what would happen next. I needed very little of actual movies as life itself was more exciting. The intensity of daily life was sometimes breathtaking. I learnt that I needed to make breaks regularly to go away and be just on my own with no outer duties. I found a rhythm of working intensely for six to eight weeks and then having a break of at least one week. During my writing time, I prolonged my stays away.

During several years, I was woken up at around four every morning. It seemed like I was easier to reach then, that there was less control on my part. I meditated and wrote and fell asleep again. Over the years I developed a kind of state of mind between meditation and sleep. During these moments I received a lot of vitalising energies, making me soft and tender. My tiredness was gone and I was ready to work again.

Today, I have arranged my bedroom, so that I am open to get refilled all night by these loving energies. This means that I need no meditation time in the morning; I have been there all night. Instead, I take my time to slowly meet the new day enjoying a long breakfast overlooking the sea. With this energy pillar within me, I am ready for a long working day.

Daily work done from this state of mind is so much easier to me than it used to be. It is there whether I do paperwork or work with companies, groups or individuals.

# INNER GUIDANCE

The veil between this physical world and the other side, or other worlds, seems to be much thinner than what most people, at least officially, admit. I have met many people, who experience the link between worlds in a very concrete fashion. But, like me, many dare not tell about these experiences, afraid of being ridiculed. In the psychotherapist's room they dare to tell about how they have clear connections with their loved ones from the other side. They speak about other lifetimes. These were stories long kept in their hearts.

In some cases, these contacts turned into a feeling of being guarded by someone from the other side. In other cases the presence from the other side was occupied with things needed to sort out to make a closure. People with the gift to see beyond the physical world are often of great help, especially when someone has died unexpectedly. They make a bridge between the worlds, and the connection is there in a different way to how most of us experience in this physical world.

**My guide**

I had felt the presence of my guide, my spiritual brother after his death. However, I was too much in control to make the link by myself in a more concrete way. A friend of mine brought me to a group session with this woman Doris. She had only met my spiritual brother once or twice in his physical life. I was the last one in the group to receive a brief clairvoyant reading session. The link was there immediately. Doris gave me messages from him that would be impossible for her to know about from other sources. Later I had an individual session and through that I gained more understanding of what was going on. So this intense inner journey started.

As I told in the first part of this book, my guide had to be very persistent to wake me up. At that time I easily let my daily busy life take over the scene. He had to really shake me up, so that I could not keep denying that he was there.

Today, I am thankful from the bottom of my heart. What he gave me was no less than the understanding of the true meaning of my life, my life purpose. Also, I finally got the answer to the inner longing I had had since I was four years old. I just ***knew*** that there was more to life than our daily life on Earth. Today, I am living this knowledge daily.

**Inner guidance changes as you grow**

To me guidance is at many levels. When you are a little child, you need different things to when you are a teenager. As a grown up you also have different needs depending on how fragile the situation is in different stages of development. The same goes for soul development as I learnt from this inner journey.

One day while driving my car on on my way to work, I saw in front of me two motorbikes. On the first one was a teenage boy, rather thin and looking young. He was proudly driving his bike and on the back was a sign "learner". Behind, and sometimes beside him, was the other bike driven by a bit older, calm and steady man. On his back was a sign of the driving school. I amazed myself by all the tears pouring down my cheeks. I was so moved by this. Here was this young man free to try himself, free to quit if he so wished, and all the time this steady, calm man was there to guide and shelter him.

This happened while I was writing this chapter and had the experience and perspective of how well I had been taken care of by my guides. I truly feel like this young man when learning how to cope with totally other worlds. I am also aware that I in other situations am the man in the back, guiding someone younger on their path of life.

This situation reminded me of a similar experience but with a much younger person being guided. I was in a ski lift queue. In front of me was a tall man and beside him a little girl of maybe four years old. It was a t-bar lift where two people go up together, standing their skies while ascending. I saw this tall man putting the board so it would fit the little girl nicely. That meant he had to put his board very uncomfortably behind his lower legs. He was obviously a good skier to be able to do this. The little girl had of course no idea of how much this guide did for her. She was just happy to go with the lift and to learn how to ski. This happened many years ago. Still I remember how my heart was pounding by this, and also how my tears came from being moved.

In the beginning I needed my guide to be very persistent, otherwise my control linked to daily life took over. Just like the little girl, I had no idea how tough that might be to someone being on the other side. My intuition tells me that there is a longing to go further, still a need to fulfil on Earth what was not completed.

**My own part of the inner guidance**

Looking back I see myself as a longing human being with clear intentions and a loving heart. Still also easily getting trapped in details of daily life, distracting me on and off. There is also a universal law saying that when you receive treasures of life it is of course wonderful *and* it also brings to the surface old blockages needing to be healed. These waves back and forth are evident when reading my manuscript.

My guides kept telling me that the start of it all was my open loving heart and my true intention that I wished to contribute to make our planet a better world to live in. My despair that night in July 2004 was my calling. And the answer came already the night after.

My guide and I had a truly loving link after sharing the same kind of life purpose for almost thirty years. There was faith and love between us that helped me get over my need for control. I understood how urgent it was that I was able to be of use as a kind of link between worlds. The co-operation between worlds was meant to integrate the wider perspectives from the other dimensions with the physical and emotional realities on Earth.

**Receiving unconditional love**

From the very beginning, I knew that what had happened to me was not for me only to enjoy or dwell in. It was for a reason as I believe it always is. For the first time in my life, I dared to fully receive unconditional love. It sounds maybe easy, but I think most of us are afraid of this, even if we are longing for it.

When I finally was able to let in the love I received from the other side, life clearly changed. Where I before used to argue, accuse or condemn, I more easily just felt tenderness. Paradoxically I found and took responsibility for my true power. No longer was I afraid of others being hurt or being envious. I knew my boundaries and naturally claimed my position. To live and let live became natural to me.

**Process pattern of guidance**

When reading my manuscript, I also trace a pattern and process of guidance. Some of those stages I think are recognised by others experiencing an inner guidance. In my case I was also brought to a master, but not until I was ready. The master was offering an etheric spiritual school, which I was brought to by my guide. I have also felt the presence of other deities receiving guidance and healing.

Here are the stages:

1. The calling
2. The knocking
3. The bridge is being confirmed
4. Being introduced to my spiritual family
5. Teaching from my cosmic home
6. Co-creation between worlds
7. Endless guidance transforming old blockages
8. Learning what Love really IS

9. To surrender means total surrender
10. Standing on my own spiritual legs
11. Manifestation in the outer world
12. A new calling to another dimension

**My guides liked to take me by surprise**

Often my guide came to me when I was the least prepared. It was as if my guides, wished to find me when I had the least control and also the least disturbance. It was very much like a radio transmission.

This is also why so much happened during the night. For long periods we met around four in the morning. I went up to another room to be by myself, made myself still and received and afterwards wrote in my diary. Then I fell asleep feeling extremely well sheltered. Later I was taken away during sleep. During the days I would often drift away in a state between meditation and sleep, sometimes only for ten or fifteen minutes. I always woke up very refreshed and filled with energy.

As I have described, my guide, my spiritual brother, was very personal and amazingly concrete in his guidance. It was as if something had to be completed in the physical world at the same time as I was to learn how to co create between worlds.

**Master K was introduced**

Without knowing anything about how life might be on the other side, my intuition told me that my guide also took steps in the realm he was. I felt clearly the importance of me staying committed also for him to be released. When I had learnt to keep the link/bridge steady, I was introduced to Master Kuthumi and his school. I found what I now call my cosmic home.

For one and a half years there were two different guiding voices. I clearly felt the different qualities. Then after 12- 13 June 2009, my first guide left. His task was completed. He had taught me enough so that I now was able to join this inner school of Kuthumi.

### Inner guidance of today

Writing this, when one and a half years have passed since my guide completed his task in June 2009, I know that this event also was a start of a new guidance and understand even more. I have no idea where this will lead me. However, I now have faith in the guidance I am receiving. And I do my best to take responsibility from my part to stay connected. This means again and again facing the old blockages that are surfacing in order to be healed. Each time the passage within me becomes clearer, new dimensions approach. It also means being alert to signals and signs when transforming the inner guidance into projects and organisations that hopefully will contribute in this world.

In the meantime I experience life extremely exciting and rich. I feel younger than I felt ten years ago, vitalised to an extent I did not know of. And I receive a lot of love in this physical life as well as the joy and excitement of creating.

### Inner guidance and my own higher self

In the view of my friend Marina, there are twelve dimensions and we all have a kind of body in each of them as well as being in our physical body here on Earth. As I myself experience that we have different energy bodies as well as our physical body, this view of Marina's comes natural to me. I guess we are just mostly unaware of our finer bodies in the higher vibrations.

So I could ask myself - who is actually the inner guide? Is it my own higher self in different dimensions guiding me here on Earth? Or is it another spirit? Maybe the whole idea of my spiritual brother guiding me has been a projection and it has it has all the time been my own higher self? Partly it might be like this. I do not know. However, the fact that I was certainly not the only one experiencing the presence of my spiritual brother, speaks for the alternative explanation that there was another energy present.

Today, to me, it does not matter. I have no need to convince anyone. I am just very thankful for what happened to me. In retrospect my intuition tells me that my inner guide was an integration on a soul level of my own higher self and the higher self of my spiritual brother. The purpose was to co-create to give directions to me living in this third dimension here on Earth.

## THE AURA - A HUMAN'S ENERGY FIELD

Some say that the human aura is the magnetic force field of the human body. Some people have the gift to actually *see* the aura, other people *feel* these kind of energies. All living things radiate a kind of energy. Recently, it has been possible to make photos of it showing that this energy field is affected by its environment, for instance by different kinds of sounds.

There are hundreds of books on this subject. However, what I know from my inner journey is that it is not enough to read *about* it. It all comes back to experiencing. I still do not know how many bodies we have as human beings. Master K told me that we have seven bodies, all related to our different openings. Examples of openings are nose, mouth, eyes, ears, navel, genital opening etc. The different chakras are also openings in the finer bodies that sometimes can be felt in our physical body, for example as a certain sensitivity in the skin. What I understood from that teaching is that our senses get more and more refined when connecting to our finer bodies. By finer I mean energies of a higher speed.

As I told before, I do not see auras. However, I clearly sense the presence of a being and, during this inner journey my inner hearing was developed immensely. When I was a child of four years old, I had my first experience of both inner sensing and inner hearing. Then I locked that door until this inner journey began. I had many other inner experiences, but not as when I was four years old.

**What is energy?**

To me - and this is today a well known fact - everything is energy. The speed of movement is just different. Also seemingly physical obstacles are energy, when you look into them. Our physical bodies are not as much kept together as we may think. There is, for instance, a lot of space between cells. We are like the stars and the planets with a lot of space in between. The scale is just different.

When I speak of "energies" in my book, I refer to those subtle energies that flow in our chakras and between other energy points. This is what is called chi in some cultures and prana in others. Western traditional medicine does not recognise this energy. However, when you yourself have experienced that quality, you cannot doubt. You just ***know.***

When we decide to commit ourselves to our spiritual inner journey, we start focusing on this subtle energy. *Energy always follows your attention and your focus.* So by focusing and practicing, this energy becomes more and more powerful. The inner connection comes to you more easily as you develop.

**The NOW moment is the entrance to eternity**

We experience heaven on earth also in our daily busy lives. Throughout the years, I have often started seminars by asking people to share the following: "Tell the person beside you about one moment in your life, when you have really felt that - yes - now I am fully alive. This moment can be from any area in your life, alone or with other people."

I have heard the most moving stories, although they had to be short in that context. "My heart was bursting with joy when I looked into the eyes of my newly born baby." "I saw the whole world in that water drop." "Being on skies in the mountain by my own was breathtaking." "We were so creative together, there was such a flow."

The list could easily fill this page and more. The next question I ask is: "How come we do not have more of these moments, when they are so precious?"

The answer is there - we forget about being in the *now moment.* Old fear and survival strategies take over. Of course we need to survive all of us. *And* we do have time to be more in the *now moment.*

So experiencing the *now moments* is the entrance to eternity. There are spiritual and meditation paths that focus mainly on that. I needed an even more concrete road to which I could really devote myself. That was the case for me also in the field of psychotherapy. Body-oriented methods, like Gestalt therapy were more attractive to me than more intellectually focussed methods. Our bodies never lie!

My training of being in the *now moment* was of great help during my inner journey. I experienced very concretely through body and sensory awareness combined with the words I got through my inner hearing. These concrete experiences were very helpful for me as I also had a very critical and controlling mind. I needed these experiences to have faith.

Master K told me to listen to the birds, to be aware of nature and be still. He told me to focus on my forehead: *"Travel with your forehead!"* Doing as he told me, I was truly flying in my inner experience. It was all about staying with that focus in the now and be aware.

Some people might say that this is not possible. To me it is an issue of practicing long enough. We all have these possibilities inside. I have now been practicing these skills intensely for seven years. It is truly like being on a training camp, always a very loving one. Sometimes it's a quite challenging one as well.

When it comes to sports, playing an instrument or learning a new language, people are often very aware that it takes time and practice to really enjoy it. Strangely enough, when it comes to the field of spirituality, I meet many who give up after their first attempt. Sometimes they even say that it does not exist, just because they themselves did not experience what they had hoped for the first time.

**The chakra system and kundalini energy**

This system is described in most kinds of religions all over the world. The terminology might be a bit different. However, the same principle is there. All the hundreds of books describing the human aura are as well describing the chakra system.

I am well acquainted with body work within psychotherapy. I have gained a lot from that to resolve old blockages for me and my clients throughout many years. Still the energy I am speaking of as "kundalini" is something else and has brought me to totally different realms.

There are many practitioners teaching about the kundalini force. In my case, it just happened through the knocking of my guide. I had not been into kundalini yoga or attended other schools to learn it. I include in this book a list of books that have been especially important to me during my inner journey. Usually, they gave me meaning *after* my own experiences. It was such a comfort to confirm that we are many on this path!

I had read about kundalini and the chakras many times earlier in my life. I believed in the concept. However, at that time I myself experienced the different chakras just vaguely. This is why I truly understand, if some people are sceptical to this concept and to an inner journey like the one I am sharing. However, I do not have the skills to play the violin. I would really love to. Still I can imagine how wonderful it would be and also all the practice behind the beautiful music.

When my kundalini opened in March 2005, I was in wonder. My reading and understanding came afterwards. I really needed books that brought this knowledge to me in a true and honest way. My sensitivity to what we call synchronicity (or what a friend of mine used as title of his book: "Chance is not a coincidence") grew more and more. In fact that was how I got the right books at the right moment. They became important teachers along the road besides my inner guidance of course.

How to experience this kundalini? Maybe this is a question from some readers, who have not yet experienced this treasure. If I knew before what I now know after this experience, I would have joined a group to study kundalini yoga or chakra meditation as a way to step-by-step get in contact with the energy that is sleeping in all of us. Well, I was not that wise, and I was lucky enough to be contacted by my guide. So to me it just happened.

**Merging energies, letting the higher energies be the Master**

Throughout this book, I have been talking about "higher energies" and "higher frequencies". This maybe sounds strange, but is in fact quite natural. The energies vibrate with a higher speed when you love than when you hate. Then you might love more or less selfless. Unconditional love, coming from a universal level, holds very high frequencies. As human beings we might have moments like this and we certainly have the potential, but we usually change back and forth concerning the frequency of energy.

When I was in Mallorca in 2007, I got an inner session from my guides teaching me about different frequencies of energy. They were skilful teachers, showing me by inspiring me to walk to two different villages, where I clearly experienced how different the quality of the frequencies were between them.

Looking back, I realise that there has been a great merging of energies within me. I learnt that the whole idea was to let the chakras holding the higher energies be the masters over the lower frequencies by merging them together. The lower energies are our survival instincts, like the needs for security, sex and power. This was taught to me step-by-step, along with how to do this in a practical way. It was not about one direction alone though. The vitality of the lower chakras was needed to fuel the fire.

Again Mallorca 2007 was a turning point to me. While writing some parts of my first book there, I was at the same time receiving session after session of concrete teaching about the kundalini energy and how it can be developed. *Do you now understand?* I heard again and again from my guides when they combined my experiences with clear instructions. I was brought into totally new worlds at the same time as I gained concrete knowledge.

By doing this daily practice over five years (and I still do of course), I was charged with an immense amount of energy. Besides being more and more vital myself, I was sheltered and guided in my daily life in a very concrete way. What in Egyptian mythology is named the "KA" (meaning our light body) was built and became like a pillar of light and energy within me, whatever I was doing in my daily life. Live and let live became easier and easier. Situations that used to upset me before did not any more. Still my boundaries were sharper than ever. This had a great impact on all my relationships, with family and friends.

Another striking experience was how these energies that were built within me through what I call "light exercises", became the prerequisite for creating new organisations, projects, writing books etc.

**The marriage between the poles**

This concept was known to me before this inner journey, but then I did not fully understand the meaning of it. I had done a lot of therapeutic work on issues like male and female parts of me as a woman. I had been a therapist working with couples for twenty-five years. Still, what happened within me on a spiritual level was totally different.

What I described before about merging different frequencies of energies valuing and needing both kinds, I call within me, "heaven and earth meet and merge." Still, there was another kind of merging of energies as well. Spiritual male and female energies have merged within me. This created a profound way of surrendering within me as it was linked to unconditional love.

During this period of time, from summer 2008 to summer 2009, I was totally overwhelmed. I had difficulties in integrating this into my daily life. I made myself lonely, too shy to share what was going on within me. Finally, I got valuable guidance from an old friend and clairvoyant lady, Marina. To her this was quite natural. She knew without me telling a word. I gained perspective and I learnt how to handle these very strong energies.

**The deeper meaning of the kundalini force**

Late evening in March 10, 2009, I got a summary of what the kundalini force is about. I got this just after the dates of 12-13 June 2009 were confirmed, and I knew that all my soul friends were able and willing to join this event.

*"There are mysteries in life that have been kept away from most people. It is about subtle energies in the encounter between worlds. It is about how sexual energy is transformed into creation, when it meets and merges with higher frequencies.*

*This is also how all kinds of true art are created. This is the deeper meaning of the kundalini force. Over time, people have distorted and perverted these energies. Time has come for more people to get in touch with this."*

What I learnt from this is that light is communication while love is creation. Love is what keeps our universe together. Without love everything falls apart.

How can we understand this while here on Earth? It all starts with an open heart wishing to be of assistance. This is what we all can do any time. This is what is happening all over the world in every moment. In a way it is very simple, still it takes courage, when we live in environments built on competition and fear, environments where the law is that of the jungle.

Applying it to the business world means that when we keep a vision beyond our own selfish needs including something good for other people, then we are working for a sustainable world. Exciting to know is that through doing this the company becomes attractive and we build long term wealthy businesses.

# FINDING YOUR LIFE PURPOSE

*"Sing your song, your own!"* These words came to me from the very beginning of my inner journey. I understood then that these words were important. Today, I understand that this is the very essence and meaning of the whole journey.

Over a period of what is soon to be forty years, I have met many people and assisted them in their struggles. The pattern emerging is to me very clear. When they were true to themselves, listening to their own little voice from inside, and also dared to make choices from that voice, then they found meaning in their lives. This path was not always an easy one. However, they found their spark of life.

The opposite was also there. Many people were not even able to find their own inner voice to begin with. They were singing the voices of other people like their parents, their spouses, their bosses, friends and others. Their lives were filled with duty, guilt and shame. Their own song was far away. These people were often depressed or suffered from other symptoms. Some of them had lost their connection with their own bodies and feelings. Their inner navigator was blocked to them.

Through psychotherapy the door to their inner spark of life was opened. Step-by-step it was possible to become a leader in their own life, to sing their own song.

Spiritually, I believe that there is an even deeper meaning to the concept of life purpose. In my view, we in another dimension somehow choose our lives. We come here to learn special aspects as well as to contribute to the learning of other people. Also, in my view, we incarnate in groups of souls with a certain purpose that we share together. This is why there is a special joy, when soul friends are coming together doing different kinds of projects. The inspiration is extremely strong, when we naturally are sharing a similar kind of life purpose.

I have had the privilege to experience this ever since I was around thirty years old. Life became extremely meaningful to me. Writing this, now being sixty-five years of age, I also understand that my life task was linked not only to the people with whom I shared a lot of love and joy. Some of the disagreements and fights I had over the years had a special meaning to me in my development. Today, I clearly thank also these people. Through our diversities, I even more learnt what my life purpose is about.

**The inner knowing**

Since I was a little child, I had always known that my life purpose was in the area of contributing to peace in the world. My parents conceived me to celebrate that World War II was over and I was born nine months later. There were no demands or visible expectations. Still there was this inner knowledge very clearly within me.

My life purpose of bringing peace does not mean that I have been more peaceful than other people, although I have always had a very open heart. Instead, this path also meant taking a position against what I used to call "silent violence". Again and again, I have found myself being rebelling against traditional views and ways of working within different parts of society like in schools, psychiatry, business etc.

The whole idea behind founding what today is the non-profit foundation Gestalt Academy of Scandinavia, was to bring in dialogue based on contact and openness into all kinds of systems in society. The aim was to contribute to peace in a practical way, not to simply talk *about* the value of peace.

From my inner journey and guidance, I understood that I was living part one of my life task from thirty years of age until the inner journey started. Today, looking back, I understand that the years of preparation was part two, the seven years of inner guidance to where I am today. Now is time for part three - to get the message out, to live my inner purpose fully.

I remember from one of the many inner sessions that I received, how I was reminded of the purpose of it all: *"Don´t think in an earthly way about this. Remember that the most important is your own life task. All codes and portals are within your bodies. They open in the speed you yourself dare to and are able to receive. This is your journey."*

In retrospect, I guess that I got this clear message, so that I would keep my focus. At that time, I was shaky and over-whelmed of what I experienced. The aim of it all was to find my life purpose, so that I could be of use.

**What is my specific purpose in this life?**

In a wider sense, I understand that I had to learn what love is and what love is not. This profound understanding was fundamental to me. I then had to apply it, my specific task. To make this very short, I would say: "Business by Heart". So my life purpose is to find ways how to bring this concept out in the world and apply it to different fields in society, not least within business itself.

Along the road, I have got and used variations of this concept. In 2005, some of my soul friends and I used the concept "Living Systems - Beholding Life Force". The vision was: *"The aim is to create meeting points for people, who work in different fields of society. What they share is a longing to be able to work in a way, so that the force of life is sustained."*

Looking back, I realise that in August 2005 I got the message about my life purpose very clearly. My guide told me: *"Don´t underestimate yourself! Thing big! You can do it, don´t ask for it - do it! You are creating a bridge between worlds and dimensions. <u>And it is about intuitive leadership in a new era.</u>*

No wonder that my challenge throughout this inner journey was to keep working as an organisational consultant on the one hand and deepening my inner journey on the other hand. If I am supposed to be a true bridge builder between business life of today and what is to come in a new era valuing heart and intuition as a guide, I need to live it through myself.

In the year of 2010, these polarities intensified. Not only did I work as an organisational consultant. I also became the managing director of the company I am part of. This happened at the same time as my inner guidance became even deeper. Facing these polarities, bringing them together, made it possible to be part of turning a crisis into flow of business. Again, I learnt from inside-out.

So now, I stand on solid ground, when I speak of business by heart. The key is an open heart, faith and trust linked to a clear-sighted reality check and honest and respectful relations.

**Conscious intention – conscious creation**

Another learning from my inner journey that I directly apply to business by heart is about conscious creation, both for individual managers and for groups and team leaders. Nowadays, I do seminars around this theme. I also apply this learning when working with team leading development especially when it comes to the issue of shared visions. It is amazing to experience a management team reach the point when from their inner driving forces they have built a shared vision. Then this vision is easily transformed into strategy and then into everyday practice. All this we have done with the company I am part of and now leading.

Being a bridge builder, I enjoy using my own learning in this way. For this purpose, I describe the steps, we practice together and the managers apply this learning in their own work. They feel safe, because I feel safe doing this. To detail how I got this learning is not the point.

**Becoming a co-creator with life**

Who is the creator in my life? What is given to me from birth and what is my own contribution?

Many people get caught in the perception of being victims. From the outside, many of us would consider some people to be truly victims. However, interestingly enough, some people stay victims all their lives, while others seem to turn even extremely heavy experiences into deep learning.

As I shared earlier, my inner truth is that we live many lives for our souls to mature. This view is also a kind of comfort, when I look at all the different kind of lives that we human beings have in common all over the planet. It does not at all take away my empathy with people living in situations of war, starvation and other situations threatened to their lives.

I do not know how I would be able to find meaning in life if I believed that only this life existed, if other dimensions did not exist. Life is to me extremely precious and valuable. I cannot believe that it all happened just by a kind of coincidence, where some people were winners and others were losers, like in a huge lottery.

Through our different kind of lives, meaning that for instance some people get old in good health while others die when they are just newborn babies, we still influence each other immensely. We learn from each other as our lives are linked together by heritance and socially. Only, I do not know what the baby would learn, if there were no other lives ahead.

Our planet is becoming smaller in the sense that we move more quickly around to all parts of the world. By this we also learn something from each other. We see pictures of starving and poor people looking at us wealthy people through the TV screen. If we do not cut off our feelings, we cannot help relating to our own lives.

It is amazing how far life often must take us, before we react in a profound way. As far our individual lives go, we often need a hit or two before we move from our comfort zone and take a new stand.

So it might be that some people suffer, for the rest of us to learn and develop. At least in that case, the suffering has not been totally in vain. Reflections like these, we need to have with a sense of timing and perspective. In the very moment of a heavy situation it needs to be taken care of. Much later, after reactions of mourning and other feelings, a new perspective might grow. I have met many clients, and other people, who have found meaning in life after great losses of dear ones. Then they have been able to turn their grief into assisting others in different ways.

The last few years I have experienced like a new wave of engagement from young people. The internet and mobiles have recently played a very important role in gathering people against violence of different kinds. To me this is very promising for the future. While writing this we have all experienced what happened in Tunis and the peaceful revolution there.

Closer to me in Stockholm, young people gathered through using the internet to take a stand against violence between young ones in the streets. As part of an older generation, remembering the 1970s, when "solidarity" was a word of honour, I feel happy and hopeful when the young ones find their ways of reacting against violence.

**Fate or free choice?**

This is a kind of duality that has been spoken about for thousands of years. What I learnt from my inner journey is that it is not an issue of either or. As I said in earlier chapter, in my view we have made a kind of outline of what to learn in our present lives. Then when living here on Earth, we continually make our choices from that seed.

Looking back, most people discover a kind of pattern in their lives. They become aware of their life choices at crossroads.

They find a "red thread" in their life pattern. It seems that there is a certain theme in life to be taken care of. It is very much like a theme in a symphony coming back in different variations. In case you have done choices in life to solve this theme, the theme has less impact later in life. Still, the theme is there and it might come as a first impulse when you need to react to something.

This is what I mean by saying that it is not about either/or. To me, free will is about how we choose to cope with our challenges.

**Co-creating with life**

The skill of co-creating is an amazing gift from my inner journey. I learnt how to create together with life instead of against life as I sometimes did before. The key is love and faith. I learnt how to differentiate between an inner state of love and faith as opposed to an inner state of survival based on fear.

To be able to co create something new, there are certain prerequisites. I learnt this hands on both from my guides and from books coming to me at the right moment. I learnt from my inner light-exercises to stay in the very moment long enough for something new to emerge. Any attempt from my part to break this due to fear, excitement or pure curiosity, immediately stopped the process. When I was able to stay in that empty void, a new kind of energy emerged, totally beyond my imagination and control.

Over the years, I received the inner light-exercises more and more easily. I had opened myself to be a total receiver of energies. Then the co-creation became like a transfusion of energies. It was like I received wisdom on an energy level to be used later in practical work.

Again, by learning myself from inside - out, I was able to apply this wisdom on a daily basis. Firstly, I learnt to apply this to fulfil my own life purpose. I became more and more alert to impulses from inside and from the world around me. Experiencing synchronicity became part of my daily living. From my perspective, this is how the business company and book was created. Synchronous events are also creating this book. The group of soul friends that we now call New Era Net was certainly created in this way.

**Ask - and you will receive**

My guides kept reminding me that nothing would have happened unless I had a clear and conscious intention myself. This is how I learnt about the great power of prayer. When we speak out loud our decree, longing and wishes from an open and loving heart, we do send out clear energy into a kind of shared force field of energy.

Carl Jung used to call this force field "the collective unconsciousness". Today, some call it the "zero point field" - a field of potential on a quantum level. These researchers suggest that this is how our brain functions, more like a radio transmitter than a producer.

To me this makes sense. One way or another, I believe that we are connected to each other in a common energy field. We know that changes seldom happen in a linear way i.e. cause-effect, but rather like a sudden "click", more of a system kind of thinking. To me we then meet on the same wavelength. This shared wavelength might be between people physically living here on Earth. It might also be between other worlds and dimensions.

When bringing my true and loving intention into our common force field of potential, new pathways in my brain are made. When I keep focusing in the direction of my true and loving intention, I build an energy momentum. Doing this, I become alert to signals going in this direction. I also influence others with that energy.

How come that you need faith and love to do this? The reason is quite simple as I learnt through my inner light-exercises. When you seek survival based on fear your focus splits, you disconnect and the creative process is blocked.

**Application to business life**

This matter of trust and faith versus survival instincts I meet over and over again within business life. Companies and organisations built on true heart-driven visions create long-term success. It is not about working without a profit. It is about being driven by heart and faith rather than by being driven by ego-driven instincts. In the latter case, your focus get disturbed and you lose the momentum of building constructive energies.

It is a pleasure to me to be able to teach and support managers and to get to know their inner state of mind. They influence a lot of people, so it means a lot that they have this awareness when making important decisions.

Often, these managers naturally have their own ways of clearing their brains from overload. It might be through sport, music or other ways of being in the very *now*. Then I also teach them how to recognise the state of mind when they get and give love. It is very simple as most of us know the feeling when we inside of us think of and see a person with whom we have experienced an exchange of love.

Being in that state of mind, a state of love and trust, it is possible to create a vision without the disturbance of fear. I then ask the managers to put the image or words on a piece of paper. Then to repeat this exercise every day for five to ten minutes. By continually focusing in this way, energy is built and new paths are made in their brains. I tell them to be alert of impulses going in the direction of their vision, impulses that probably would not have been noticed otherwise.

This wisdom coming from my inner journey, was the leading message of my former book "The Power of Trust – In a World of Sharp Elbows". At that time, I wrote without sharing my actual source of wisdom. In my inner knowing, this was wisdom from Egyptian mythology applied to today's business life. However, modern understanding from neuroscience is in essence saying the same thing using other words. So I got another way of explaining how we co create with life.

What I received and what we cannot get from *reading* about it are the actual skills how to do it. I am now trained, it comes naturally and is a part of my living. Because of this, I can easily teach it to others.

## NEW ERA NET

Over the years of my inner journey, I was aware of the fact that I was being prepared to be able to organise a kind of school assisting people to deal with the challenges in entering a new era.

I was told through my inner learning, that we all will need a set of tools and skills that have not been valued in our present society. These tools are in essence not new. On the contrary, indigenous people all over the planet have kept these tools as necessary wisdom keepers. All over the world, now we finally are learning from them so that we will be able to integrate their wisdom into our modern society. Why are these skills and talents especially needed today? We might use different words, but I clearly see that most of us agree that we need to be driven by our hearts - not only by our intellect. Our society has seen great technical and medical progress, but we have not at all matured as human *beings* in the same speed. This means that we in fact keep very dangerous toys in the hands of people who are not mature enough to handle them in a wise way.

Talking *about* peace and sustainability is quite easy and the conferences on these themes are many. To make it happen in reality, we need to practice. We need to face how we in practice are handling diversities of different kinds. We need to have the courage to build on trust and faith, when we cooperate with each other.

What I learnt from my inner journey is how much easier. I am able to stay in faith and trust when I am supported from within.

In turn, when I am able to stay in faith and trust, I influence and inspire others to do the same.

I also learnt the great power of when a group of people commit themselves to build their common work on trust and faith. Even more, when each of the members of a group devotes themselves as receivers of guidance from other dimensions, then a very intense energy is built on a group level. This is what happened as a first step in February 2009 in Den Haag and later as a completion and a new beginning in June 2009 in Stockholm.

Preparing for the event in Den Haag, when the seeding of the becoming School was made, I got the following inspiration on 24 January 2009:

A Mystery School of Our Time.

The mysteries of life cannot be understood unless we investigate using our whole being as an instrument. Our senses, our feelings, our consciousness are the tentacles, when a soul is finding its way home. Each of us has their own journey. Every journey is unique. Each of us has their own understanding making it within their own context.

We wish to offer useful tools for this inner journey, powerful and healthy tools to assist everyone to find their spark of life. A Mystery School of Our Time does not teach a certain religion. It's important however to keep an open mind and longing for an inner journey.

The power of creation is within each of us. It is about discovering how this force can be used for purposes to serve the wholeness and our Earth.

There are different entrances and paths for each of us.

**Meeting in Den Haag, February 2009 - we have sown the seeds**

With the assistance of my friend Doris, the three of us who met were able to understand and sow the very seed of the becoming school. As I wrote in the first part of this book, we were contacted about a month before by my guide, my spiritual brother. It was during the same night at about half past three in the morning. The day after, all was settled.

During the days in Den Haag, we meditated together, sharing our inner experiences. Also, Doris gave readings using her gift of clairvoyance. New to me during these days, was our shared experience of the thin veil between the dimensions. I had my own experiences long held within myself. Experiencing this together was special. I trembled from love and excitement. My heart knew this to be true and my intellect had to go to rest.

We recorded all sessions. At night I wrote everything down for future reference and for us to see the pattern understanding the message given to us. Our part of the co-operation was to transform this into everyday practice.

I had not shared with Doris about the content of my inspiration a month earlier. She spoke in symbols. Within her she "saw" my spiritual guide and clearly heard his words. So the connection as well as the instructions were there:

*"The building of the temple has now started. Temples can be so different. It does not have to be a building but <u>A temple of our time</u>. Just as when you build a wall, we are building this temple stone, by stone or you could say moment by moment – Barbro is holding the trowel in her hand."*

Doris found this image to be quite amusing. I realised that my life purpose in this was to keep my special link with my guide and thereby learn how to interpret some of the symbols or even rebuses given to us. I was also the one to organise and hold the project together.

**Inspiring my soul friends to meet in Stockholm, 12-13 June 2009**

This period of my inner journey was exciting to the point of being feverish. After all these years being mainly on my own in my inner journey, it was now time to manifest as a group of souls.

I had moments when I asked myself if this was really true. Still the amount of energy that was raised, all the inner sessions and the sharing with my friends on this path, told me that we all were part of something special.

The people to meet in Stockholm were truly no beginners. We were all in our different ways skilled and experienced people. All seven of us had our own specific spiritual path and tasks. Four of us were, like me, bridge-builders within our different professions, while three had devoted their professional lives totally to the spiritual realm being well-known teachers and guides. So we were there with different tasks in our joint venture.

When during March 2009 I finally understood that the event in Stockholm would happen, I was, of course, full of joy. At the same time, I needed help to be able to handle this in connection with my daily life. Not until I met with Marina did I find peace within.

**Completion and beginning 12-13 June 2009.**

When I read my notes from these two days, they are very short. It was like I was not able to speak. Today, one and a half years later, I am able to share a bit more.

I realise now, that the main reason for us to meet as a group, was to build enough energy for the transmission to happen. There was an exchange of energies between the worlds even more intense than in Den Haag some months earlier. We were all necessary co-creators for this to happen. Some of the others were more experienced than I. They held the energy for us and together with us for the manifestation to happen.

As a group, we received a lot on an energy level. Now, it was up to us to find ways how to express this in practice here on Earth.

**Manifesting into this world**

When we were in Den Haag, I received the name: "The New Era College" for our shared project. None of us was thinking of a concrete building as in a traditional college. We imagined a kind of non-profit organisation offering seminars etc. Today, reflecting on the process of bringing our gift from an energy level into a concrete project, I realise that at least I, and maybe some of my friends, were caught in the old way of thinking about what an organisation is.

The first year after the event in June 2009, four of us prepared for the creation of a non-profit organisation. We were what I call "bridge-builders" in the group. We wished to translate the message into everyday practice, assisting people in their own environments.

We are all capable and organised people, used to doing things like this. But, somehow, the time was not right for this kind of expression. Instead each of us met our deepest fears. We assisted each other in this and also in each our professional fundament for living and creating. We deepened our relationships as friends on this path.

In June 2010, exactly a year after the event in Stockholm, the four of us met with my friend Marina. Again, we gathered on a group level, again the energy level was raised. We got the necessary instructions.

Then during autumn 2010, in parallel with my friends, I found that we had been blocking the energy as we were caught in old, conventional thinking. My own inner learning was necessary for understanding. Afterwards, this seems so simple. If we wish to bring a new way of organising things into this world, of course we need to do it ourselves first.

My part of this, I found out, was that I had been holding back my leadership by hiding in the group. Of course, this was blocking the others as well. Each of us has to be our own energy pillar when bringing out our messages. It was evident that we - at least for now - do not need a formal organisation for this new school. That might even be perceived as excluding the people we wish to connect with.

Now, I feel free to be the energy pillar of a network of independent organizations and people. We call this network the *New Era Net*. My vision is that today, we are not in the need of new "schools" in a traditional sense. What we need is to come together and make visible all the different paths people are undertaking in order to bring peace and sustainability to our planet.

Bringing together here and there groups of people, who in their own ways share the same kind of longing and wish for the Earth, will multiply many times the energy we all are investing. Eventually, I believe that this will change also old structures that now keep the formal power on Earth.

**Concrete projects**

How many times do I need to discover, that when I am stuck out there, it is always due to me being stuck inside? Now the flow is there in the New Era Net. This is expressed in the work each of us are doing within our daily professional lives. It is also expressed in concrete projects now and ahead. We let each project be independent in terms of responsibilities and economy. We are on our way now, having faith in the process.

For many reasons, linked also to other dimensions, there is a bridge now built, especially between our friend Justo from Bolivia to the rest of us living in Europe. To the public, this is right now expressed as a seminar on "Visionary Medicine". This seminar is held by the three pioneers in this field: Johannes, Justo and Marie.

I will bring worlds together by introducing Marina and Justo to each other. Somehow, I wish them to meet. Most of us in the group will join in this in June 2011. Ahead of me are also two special journeys, one to Tibet in May 2011 and one to Bolivia and Peru in October 2012. They are milestones along my path. I know them to be essential for my life task ahead.

In the meantime, in my daily life, I keep working within business life being an organisational consultant and an MD in the company I am part of. Today, there is a flow within me, when I am living the title of my book: "Head in Heaven, Feet on the Ground, Hands in Society."

"Head in Heaven" means to me that we need this kind of inspiration so that we are able to keep an open heart, bringing this state of mind into our daily lives. In turn this is what is needed to bring harmony to our planet.

**...."forget your perfect offering"...**

What can each of us do to bring our planet into harmony? Well, that question was the start of my whole inner journey. My conclusion is:

*We do not have to know.*

We need to bring our true intention from our open hearts. We need to ask for help, when we get blocked or afraid in other ways.

Coming together in groups from open hearts, is very powerful. We need to be open enough so that we recognise our longings and wishes, like beacons on the sea. This is one reason why I am writing this book. It is a bit like waving with a flag. We are many waving out there.

We all know that besides open hearts we are all also parts of destructiveness of different kinds. In spite of lots of darkness around the world, I am still hopeful. That is why I keep quoting the words in the song "Anthem" by Leonard Cohen:

“Ring the bells that still can ring,
Forget your perfect offering.
There is a crack in everything,
That´s how the light gets in,
That´s how the light gets in.“

Let´s ring together…..

## BOOKS AND LYRICS

These books and lyrics came to me during my inner journey, becoming inspiring teachers in the right time.

Redfield, James: *Secret of Shambhala.*
Gave me inspiration and structure for my first steps.

Cohen, Leonard: *Anthem* from the album *Future.*
Inspired me how to breathe in light and unconditional love.

Heartsong, Claire: *Anna, Grandmother of Jesus.*
Made my longing ever stronger.

Kuthumi: *Teachings for the New Golden Age.*
Made me feel finally at home.

Kuthumi and Djawl Kul: *The Human Aura.*
*How to Activate and Energize your Aura and Chackras*
Gave me a deep understanding through recognizing and bringing in the bigger picture.

Kenyon, Tom and Essene, Virginia: *The Hathors.*
Gave me a structure linked to my experiences, confirming my inner connection to Egyptian mysteries.

Kenyon, Tom and Sion, Judi: *The Magdalene Manuscript.*
Came to me as a precious gift, when I was totally on my own, recognizing, understanding.

Padma Aon Prakasha: *The Nine Eyes of Light.*
Came to me in the process of publishing giving me overview and strength.

# SPECIAL THANKS!

It has taken a whole crew to give birth to this book. I have been surrounded by my loving family, letting me be who I am, wishing me well in my journeying. I am surrounded by friends and colleagues who I feel are with me also in times like this when I make myself vulnerable. Thank you all! Your support has been like open arms.

In the special task of producing this book I still like to acknowledge some people who have had their unique part in this project.

*Jorge Rosner*
Meeting you as my first teacher within Gestalt theory and methodology when I was thirty years old, became a turning point in my life. You inspired me especially through your skilful application of Zen Buddhism and Existentialism, the spiritual and philosophical roots of Gestalt. These tools have been my foundation when journeying into other dimensions. So your gift is to me even clearer today.

*Doris Ankarberg*
Your accurate clairvoyant readings over five years were necessary for me to be able to have faith in and develop my own inner hearing and sensing. You were by my side all the way until completion. I am forever deeply thankful!

*Marina Munck*
I came to you twice when I was in great need and for special purposes. Your clear sight, integrity and warm heart made me totally calm and free to go on. My heart is with you always! And I keep learning from you for my new beginnings.

*Marie Örnesved*
Being my publisher you opened yourself to enter the room of my book. You have been doing this in a concrete, skilful and loving way. Like a midwife you have supported me in giving birth to my book. Quite a job after me being on my own for seven years!

*Åsa Rosén*
How to get fresh peonies in March in Sweden? No problem for you, you just imported them! You also found a skilful photographer, whom you inspired for this project. This is you, full of talent, love and vitality! You are such a gift to me designing my book.

*Mikael Curman*
I dedicate my book to you. All these years, you have been my shelter while I have been journeying between worlds. You have given me the freedom to fulfil my life purpose. That is to me the greatest way of loving me. I wish the same to you!

www.ingramcontent.com/pod-product-compliance
Ingram Content Group UK Ltd.
Pitfield, Milton Keynes, MK11 3LW, UK
UKHW062309290726
14090UKWH00018B/969